Daily Living With a Handicapped Child

DIANA M. MILLARD

CROOM HELM
London & Canberra

© 1984 Diana M. Millard
Croom Helm Ltd, Provident House, Burrell Row,
Beckenham, Kent BR3 1AT
Croom Helm Australia Pty Ltd, 28 Kembla Street,
Fyshwick, ACT 2609, Australia

British Library Cataloguing in Publication Data

Millard, Diana M.
    Daily living with a handicapped child.
    1. Handicapped children — Care and treatment
    I. Title
    362.4'088054   HQ773.6
    ISBN 0-7099-1701-5

Printed and bound in Great Britain by
Spottiswoode Ballantyne Ltd., Colchester and London

DAILY LIVING WITH A HANDICAPPED CHILD

CROOM HELM SPECIAL EDUCATION SERIES
Edited by Bill Gillham, Child Development Research Unit,
University of Nottingham

Already Available:

ENCOURAGING LANGUAGE DEVELOPMENT
Phyllis Hastings and Bessie Hayes

INDEPENDENCE TRAINING FOR VISUALLY HANDICAPPED
CHILDREN
Doris W. Tooze

WORK PREPARATION FOR THE HANDICAPPED
David Hutchinson

TOYS AND PLAY FOR THE HANDICAPPED CHILD
Barbara Riddick

TEACHING POOR READERS IN THE SECONDARY SCHOOL
Christine Cassell

TEACHING READING TO MENTALLY HANDICAPPED CHILDREN
James Thatcher

DAILY LIVING WITH A HANDICAPPED CHILD
Diana M. Millard

Contents

Series Foreword

The Croom Helm Special Education Series is explicitly intended to give experienced practitioners in the helping services the opportunity to present a wide range of remedial programmes and techniques which they have developed in practice. The basis of the editorial policy is the belief that there exists much 'good practice' which warrants wider dissemination in book form. The present project is, therefore, concerned with the communication of ideas and methods developed by those who use them in their working lives.

Daily Living With A Handicapped Child deals, in an essentially practical fashion, with the daily problems of care posed by a handicapped child in a family and the emotional and social difficulties that are part of that special situation. It is a handbook for parents themselves and for the many professionals who support parents in meeting their children's special needs.

B.G.

Preface

This book is intended for the parents of a handicapped child and for those members of a wide range of professions who advise and assist them in the day-to-day care of their child. From the moment the parents are told that there is something 'wrong' with their child — and the manner of the telling has vast implications for their future handling of him — they need continuous support, reassurance and practical guidance.

Many parents of normal children experience difficulties of management. Generally speaking, Westernised society lacks the basic education in caring for children which, in some cultures, is provided incidentally by large or extended families. Where there are several children in a family, the older ones are helping to care for the younger ones, who then take their turn in the care of nephews and nieces. Similarly, in the extended families found in many societies there are always young children to be tended, so that the young people learn about child care by experience. The modern 'nuclear' family does not provide such opportunities to practise child rearing 'under supervision' before having children of one's own.

Another problem is that because of social, educational and geographical mobility, young couples are apt to live some distance away from their own parents or to feel that their attitudes to child rearing differ. As a result they may face the problems of parenthood without the support of their own parents, or indeed of anyone of a previous generation. How much greater are the implications for the parents of a handicapped child? Their isolation and need for support is the more serious because even the advice of other parents of their own age may not be relevant to the care of their special child.

Because each child is an individual, and the nature, range and effect of a handicapping condition can vary greatly in degree from one child to another, the practical advice offered in this book should be interpreted in conjunction with detailed assessment of the child's personal requirements.

CHAPTER 1

A Special Baby

When parents have been told that their child is handicapped, the range and nature of their reactions can be very varied. The initial shock may cause negative attitudes such as anger and resentment or a detached feeling of helplessness, and may be followed by a period of grief. The parents will experience fears for the future, fear of the effects that the handicapped child will have on them and the rest of the family, and fear as to their ability to cope with all the demands which may be put upon them. Since individuals react in different ways to this kind of stress, it may be that one parent can deal with the present problems better than the other at various times. If this is the case, then that partner must be aware of the need to give extra support to the other at this time, and be willing to receive such comfort in turn. Mutual support and positive attitudes will lead to a constructive approach to the situation, and all speculation concerning cause and blame should be shelved in favour of looking to the future.

The handicapped child is a member of the family, therefore his future and that of the other members are interdependent. The early stages are not the time for making long-term decisions, but the time for the parents to get to know their child and to come to terms with the fact of his handicap. It is probable that the doctors involved have not given a very clear picture of how the child will develop. This is because it is not always possible to forecast the effect of certain conditions. For example, the extent of damage may not be detectable in a very young child, and in the case of many well-known conditions the degree of severity may not be clear. It also has to be borne in mind that new methods of treatment are frequently being discovered and one of these may be appropriate for the child at some stage in his life. Two major factors in determining the outcome of a child's condition will be his family's attitude to him, and the use made of available professional advice and services. To this must be added the personality of the child, which affects not only his own progress but the attitude of others towards him. As the child grows older, his potential abilities may become more predictable, but in principle his future should be met one step at a time.

The most natural place for a baby in our society is in his own home, being cared for by his own family. Professionals may have plenty of knowledge and experience to pass on, but it is the parents who will care for and teach their baby, and who have the special commitment that comes from close emotional involvement. All parents are vulnerable through such involvement but this vulnerability is greater for the parents of a handicapped child. Normal hopes and expectations are replaced by uncertainty and it may be that the parents are afraid to risk too much of themselves. But their commitment is indispensable to the handicapped child. In fact, most of his needs are the same as those of any other baby. The chief difference may be only that his needs last longer.

Although many fathers successfully assume the mothering role when circumstances are appropriate, in our society today the person who normally has the closest involvement with a baby is his natural, adoptive or foster mother. She is the first person the baby gets to know, his first contact with other people and his major link with them. She is with him at his times of greatest enjoyment, the times when he wakes up, feeds, is bathed, and falls asleep. She cares for him when he is hungry, tired or troubled, and her place in his life is unique. Since it is therefore on her that most of the problems of daily living fall, it is for her that the greater part of this book has been written.

Caring for the Baby

From the moment she holds him in her arms, mother and baby have a special relationship. Although many mothers are cautious in their handling of a newborn baby, confidence soon develops as she learns to love, handle and communicate with him. If there is nothing to hinder her, she soon learns to trust her own judgement and instinct. The knowledge that a baby is handicapped can inhibit that natural process. It is important that a mother should not be afraid of caring for her child, as it is most unlikely that she can harm him in any way. Of course, some of the things a mother can do for her baby may be more beneficial than others, but the worst thing that could happen to either of them would be for her to be so fearful of doing the wrong thing that she ends up not doing anything for him at all. The mother whose first baby is handicapped is particularly vulnerable in this respect. She needs to be reassured that many of the difficulties she may encounter in caring for her handicapped baby are the same as those she might find in any baby.

If the family is to continue to live a normal life, and give a normal life to the handicapped child, there are certain steps that must be taken immediately. The first step is perhaps the hardest one. Family, friends and neighbours must be told about the child and his handicap. Although his parents may still be very upset themselves, it is essential that they put everyone else in the picture straight away. Unless this is done early, the challenge it represents will grow threatening. It will be necessary to decide on the best way to tell them, bearing in mind that it will be a shock for *them*. This is a time when openness brings great benefits since it will evoke offers of help and support which might otherwise be withheld for fear of encroaching. The family that isolates itself is in danger of increasing its internal stress.

Once people have come to terms with the situation, they will begin to offer advice. All of it will be well-intentioned, but much of it is sure to be conflicting. Sifting the helpful from the useless applies not only to such personal advice but also to the advice available from professional workers and from books. Parents need to use their common sense to sort out the advice and information they are given, and then to decide on their own way of doing things, based on this and on their own feelings and experience. Only they can know how something will work out in their present situation. An 'expert', that is a person with specialist knowledge in a particular field, is likely to be a more reliable source of advice and information than friends and neighbours. Making the best use not only of hospital staff but also of such people as the bank manager, marriage guidance counsellor and others, is a skill that the parents of a handicapped child may need to develop to a high degree.

For problems concerned directly with the child's condition, the advice of a doctor should be sought. It may well be that there is no specific treatment either available or advisable for the child at this stage in the way of drugs, operations or exercises. However, this does not mean that nothing can be done for him. What it does mean is that no specialist equipment or skill is required, and that the baby can best be helped to develop by his own family and in his own home.

Stimulating the Baby

With the exception of babies suffering from conditions such as *osteogenesis imperfecta* ('brittle bones', see p. 14) all handicapped babies need to be handled, moved and cuddled in the normal way. They need to hear voices, music and other sounds, and to see bright colours, moving objects and familiar faces. The baby must be stimulated in as many ways as possible right from the beginning, and this process can be an enjoyable one for all the family. It is essential to be aware that a 'good' baby, who lies quietly in his pram or cot and never cries, needs far more handling and talking to than a normal baby in order to arouse his senses.

As a general rule the baby should not be allowed to lie on his back. Not only is there the danger of his inhaling vomit, but there are several positive reasons why other positions are more beneficial. He should be laid on his side, and turned on to the other side each time he has been fed and changed. Side-lying has the advantage of enabling him to see objects close to him, thereby teaching him to focus his gaze; the ceiling is far away from a supine child, and is usually bare and white. It also has the advantage of bringing both his hands near to his face without his having to lift them against gravity. This is of special importance since the co-ordination between hands and eyes, so necessary for manipulation, begins at this very early stage. By bringing his knees together also, this position is vital to babies whose muscles are weak and whose limbs are floppy, as it will help to prevent the ligaments surrounding their hip joints from becoming stretched. Lying on alternate sides will help to mould the shape of the head evenly, and for breast-fed babies is quite a useful way of remembering which breast to offer first at the next feed. Prone-lying (lying on the stomach) is often advocated and is an alternative to side-lying. It should not be used for floppy babies as it encourages slack hips, limits kicking, and prevents manipulation; but its use is essential during sleeping times for children with cerebral palsy who show a tendency to cross their legs. If the baby seems to roll from his side on to his back rather easily, it is helpful to make a soft roll measuring about 15 inches long and 4 inches in diameter out of a spongy material. When the baby is put on his side, positioning this roll close against his back before he is covered up should be sufficient to stop him from rolling over.

When the baby is wakeful, the mother should keep him with her as much as possible. If he has learnt to hold his head up then he can be carried in a sling while she gets on with some of the chores. If he has cerebral palsy he will benefit from straddling his mother with his legs. However, a baby with Down's syndrome should not be carried in this way as his legs must be kept together. If the baby has not yet learnt head control, he can be sat in a reclining chair with his head supported, and the chair placed at an angle from which he can watch his mother with ease. The chair should not be left on the floor, which is draughty and boring, but fastened securely to a dining chair, table or work top so that **he** can see his mother's face. Then she can talk to him as she works, touch him as she passes by, and give him things to look at and hold. Such stimulation is vital to his development, even when the baby does not appear to respond. While a normal baby will kick and squirm, wave his hands about and try to lift his head without encouragement, the handicapped baby has to be taught to make these movements, for unless he does his handicap will have a greater effect on him. He may give less response than a normal baby would, and this can be disheartening, but after persevering for a while the mother will find that this special interaction becomes so natural that she will be stimulating him effortlessly.

Feeding

Whether the baby is breast-fed or bottle-fed, the sensations experienced by both mother and infant at feeding times should be pleasurable. Feeding is a profoundly significant form of social interaction, which requires much thought and preparation to make it effective. As with a sophisticated dinner party, the

atmosphere is important. The mother should make sure that she feeds her baby in a warm and restful atmosphere and that she is as relaxed as possible. It is worth making a deliberate attempt to avoid interruptions and interference, helpful or not. This is a time when the mother needs to be able to give her baby her undivided attention. Everything needed should be collected together, within reach, before she starts to feed him. Sitting on a comfortable chair, she should hold her baby close to her in such a way that he is as upright as possible, not just lying across her lap. Because feeding is a time when mother and baby should communicate, which is very important for the baby's happiness and development, he should never be fed at arm's length or with his mother's attention divided in any way.

The quality of the interaction is more important than all the arguments about breast versus bottle-feeding. If the mother enjoys breast-feeding and the baby is thriving, that is fine. But if the mother doesn't enjoy it or the baby does not seem to be making good progress, or she can't cope with it for any reason, then it should be abandoned. There are so many excellent substitutes on the market that, provided feeds are prepared properly and the normal precautions of hygiene are observed, it does not matter whether the child is bottle or breast-fed. The main risk of bottle-feeding is infection, but as long as the rules for sterilising the equipment are followed and only water which has been boiled is used, there should be no problems. It is never wise to prop a bottle up in the baby's mouth, and it shouldn't be given back to him if it has been dropped without first cleaning the teat.

As most babies will take over half the food they want in the first few minutes, there is little point in spending the best part of an hour trying to coax them to take more food. Twenty minutes is a reasonable time. However, if the mother thinks that her baby hasn't taken enough then she can give him his next feed earlier. Little and often may be best for lazy babies or those with small appetites. Every effort should be made to fit feeding times to the baby rather than to an imposed routine and to feed him more or less on demand, provided that feeds are not more than four hours apart initially. 'Good' babies who don't demand frequent feeds put themselves at risk, so in their case a timetable, rather than feeding on demand, *is* necessary. From what we know about intellectual development at this stage, it is reasonable to say that babies under six months of age cannot be 'spoilt' or 'taught to wait' over the matter of feeding.

Introducing solids by two or three months of age is very worthwhile as delay can cause problems later on. At about this time the baby can be offered drinks such as fruit juice or boiled water in a spouted cup. Both spout and spoon will be disliked at first, but the baby is being given an early opportunity to get used to them. Breast or bottle can be gradually phased out as the baby begins to tolerate the cup. This is achieved more easily if he is offered a drink only from a cup at alternate feeds, and then more often so that he is only having a breast or bottle feed in the evening after the rest of his meal. A reasonable aim is to have ceased breast and bottle feeds by the age of about nine months.

The establishment of a routine can be quite difficult with a very young baby when the mother is trying to feed on demand, but may be essential in enabling her to cope with her daily tasks. Most mothers find that a bath at about nine o' clock in the morning, followed by a feed at about ten o' clock is a convenient time to centre the routine on. They then work backwards or forwards from there. If feeds occur approximately four-hourly, they could take place at about 6.00 a.m., 10.00 a.m., 2.00 p.m., 6.00 p.m. and 10.00 p.m., with or without a night feed at 2.00 a.m. This is fine if the baby has developed a regular pattern and his father does not come off shift work at 2.00 p.m. or arrive home for a meal soon after 6.00 p.m. In these cases it would probably be easier to feed the baby at times centred on 9.00 a.m. and either bath him before that feed, or bath him in the evening. If the baby is being fed three-hourly, the mother will have rather a tight schedule and will need to plan her day in greater detail. However, it should always be remembered that routines are designed only to make life easier for both mother and baby. Such rules are not sacrosanct and may need to be modified on some occasions.

Feeding the Older Baby

Feeding an older baby can be easier in many respects. For one thing, he does not have to be fed so often. Three meals a day, and an evening drink, will usually be sufficient. However, this is often the stage at which children start to develop likes and dislikes and to display an occasional fad. This is where parental ingenuity is put to the test. If the child takes a dislike to a certain food, it has to be decided whether or not that food could be omitted from his meals. Many fruits and vege- tables are interchangeable in terms of nourishment, so one can easily be substi- tuted for another. There is no point in unnecessary battles. Unfortunately, there are certain essential foods for which there is no substitute, and these cannot be excluded from the diet. However, the majority can be disguised in some way. For example, if the baby will no longer drink milk it has to be made more attrac- tive for him, perhaps by adding a little milk shake syrup to it. If this does not disguise it enough, he can be given fruit juice or water to drink; the milk can be offered in the form of custard, blancmange, junket and so on. If he won't eat boiled eggs, they can be offered scrambled, mashed, whisked in milk or added to custard, or even in the form of French toast. Imagination is the main way to overcome these problems, and it is important to think in this strategic way rather than to let worries develop. The most important thing is to prevent meal-times from becoming battle-grounds. 'Force-feeding' is not good for the child or his mother, and the use of a little cunning will save a great deal of anxiety and tension.

Day-to-day Care

Bath-time

A baby bath is probably one of the earliest pieces of equipment parents buy when shopping for their baby. However, it may not be the ideal method of bathing a baby. The idea of setting it up in the nursery and carrying heavy buckets for filling and emptying is really a throwback to Victorian times when there was no water on tap; before going through all that complicated procedure, it is worth considering the alternatives. Provided it can be warmed adequately, any room will do. The obvious room to use if other factors permit is the bathroom. It may be possible to erect the baby bath and its stand in the big bath, as long as it is very firm and there is no danger of its slipping. If it isn't safe, a rubber mat in the bottom of the big bath will do the trick, or the baby bath can perhaps be lashed to the taps or to any handles which are incorporated in the sides of the bath. Failing this, it may be possible to obtain a 'Swedish bath grip' from the occupational therapy department at the local hospital. This is a handle which clamps on to the side of most baths, and it may give a good anchorage at which to tie the baby bath. Using the big bath in this way the baby bath can be filled by means of a hose, and since most are nowadays fitted with a plug, emptying will be no problem. Another alternative is to bath the baby in the kitchen sink. If rubber nozzle ends are fitted to the taps, the baby will not be hurt by accidentally knocking them. The draining board then becomes a useful place on which to lay the baby while his face and hair are washed and while his nappy is removed and he is soaped. Never let go of the baby on the draining board or, indeed, on any other surface apart from the floor. If the bathroom boasts a bidet a very small baby might be bathed in that for a time.

Once the child has outgrown his baby bath or the sink, he progresses to the big bath. If he can sit up without support there will be few problems. However, when he is being washed the mother should kneel down beside the bath if she is to avoid backache. If he has to be held because he cannot sit up, there are a few useful aids. A shallow-bath will be most useful as the child grows bigger. Moulded from very light material, it sits firmly on a conventional bath and reduces its depth. The child can lie in it without adult support, and he can easily be reached. Alternatively there is an inflatable chair in which the child can sit in the bottom of the bath, or the 'Bath Care Chair' which also leaves the adult's hands free to wash him. All these are available through an occupational therapist, and if none of them answers a particular need, she can suggest other alternatives.

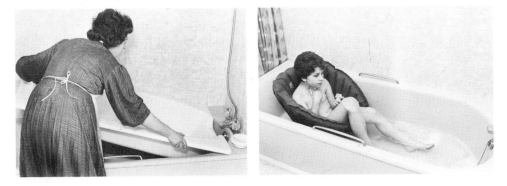

Before preparing a baby for his bath, it is important to collect together all that will be required. If there is not enough space to store everything in the room in which he is bathed, then it is worth investing in a sturdy trolley and keeping all the equipment on that. This will save endless journeys from room to room, and the risk involved in leaving the child unattended while some forgotten article is fetched.

Nappy-folding

There are various methods of folding nappies and for most babies one method is as good as another. However, for babies suffering from certain conditions, the

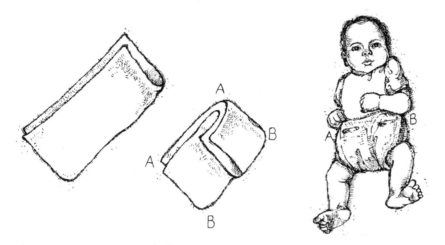

way they wear a nappy can help to overcome some of their problems. One of the most common conditions requiring a special method of folding the nappy is that known as 'clicking hips' (see p. 13). The doctor will advise that the nappy is folded lengthwise and fastened with two pins. The baby may also have to wear a plastic 'envelope splint' over his nappy. This simple treatment is often enough to

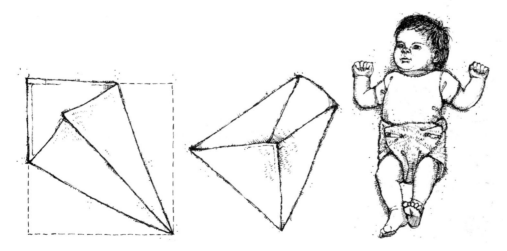

cure the condition, although the method has to be used for some months. The wide nappy is also useful in controlling the baby who has a tendency to cross his legs, such as a baby suffering from cerebral palsy (see p. 41) who has strong adductor muscles, as it keeps his legs well apart.

Another way to fold a nappy is by the 'kite' method. This shape provides a thick, narrow portion between the legs, and pulls the legs forward and together. It is therefore excellent for babies suffering from Down's syndrome, and for all other 'floppy' babies. Its width can be varied according to the size of the baby, and tucking in the slight fullness at the sides makes the baby look neat. There are no large lumps of nappy between the legs to chafe, and soiling is confined to a small area. It is fastened by two pins.

For the premature or very thin baby, a third method can be used. It results in a small triangle with plenty of thickness between the legs, and is fastened with one pin.

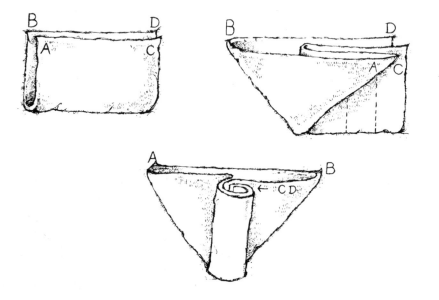

The most common way of folding nappies is into a large triangle. The top point is brought up between the baby's legs, each side is then wound round underneath him, and the lower point is drawn up and pinned. This means a great deal of bulk between the legs and under the buttocks. Soiling affects almost the entire nappy, and the result is usually very untidy. Add to this the fact that the baby has to sit or lie on rather a lumpy bundle, and it is clearly not very satisfactory. The kite method is preferable.

The use of a liner limits much of the soiling of the nappy. However, most of the nappy liners available are very thin and not particularly absorbent. The best way of dealing with this is to buy disposable nappy pads or a disposable roll, and to cut pieces up to insert in the ordinary nappy. When the baby is very small, a piece of disposable pad measuring about four inches wide and eight inches long laid in the nappy will contain most of the soiling, and as he grows bigger the size of the pieces used can be enlarged. Changing the baby on her lap is not difficult and ensures that the mother has absolute control of him.

Bed Time

Whether a baby goes to sleep quickly and happily or not depends a great deal on the way he is prepared for bed. If he is rushed or the mother tries to deal with something else at the same time, or there is too much going on around him, he may become over-stimulated and will find it difficult to settle. The desirable situation is to give plenty of time to creating a quiet, warm and relaxed atmosphere. Murmuring and singing to him as he is undressed and fed will help to create calmness. Dim lights in his bedroom continue this atmosphere as does laying him gently in his cot and tucking him in firmly. The light should then be switched off and the door pulled to. If there is a light outside his room, that should also be switched off so that he cannot see any shapes or shadows. There is no need to go about on tiptoe or to keep the radio or television off; it is better for the baby to learn to sleep in background noise than in complete silence, so that a passing car or a closing door are less likely to startle him.

It is quite normal for a baby to lie awake for some time. Peeping in at him to see if he is asleep will only rouse him and make it more difficult for him to drop off. However, if he will not lie quietly when he is put down and is clearly not ready for sleep, then he can be taken back into the living room and positioned where he can watch what is going on, but he should not be fussed over. Babies who have a late feed at ten or eleven o'clock in the evening need not go to bed until their parents do. There are no rules to say that babies must be put in their bedrooms after tea: some families have only one room in which to live.

If the baby has to be fed during the night, it is a good idea for the mother to make a hot water bottle when she gets up. This can be put into the baby's cot as soon as he is picked up, and the covers pulled over it. He should be fed and changed in dim light to avoid over-stimulating him, and when he is put back to bed the hot water bottle should be removed, leaving the bed warm and relaxing. If the baby is a very poor sleeper, the doctor may advise a mild sedative, which should be used, as the other members of the family should be given the opportunity to get their proper rest.

Going to bed should never be used as a punishment, as it will cause endless problems at normal bedtimes. After the baby has been tucked up, his mother should spend a few seconds whispering to him so that the last thing he sees and hears before sleeping is her.

The Baby's Health

A baby with a handicapping condition can still be healthy if he is kept clean, warm and free from infection. Unless there is medical advice to the contrary, he should receive all the inoculations against infectious diseases that are offered to normal children, and at the same age. The baby has enough to contend with in his handicap; it is important to ensure that he is as fit as possible in all other respects.

If the baby has to take medicine in some form it must be administered with care. He should always be given the exact dose at the exact interval. If for any reason a dose is omitted, it should never be given in a double quantity the next time. It is important to make a note of the name of the drug, to keep labels intact, and not to transfer pills or medicines to other containers. Without this sort of discipline it is easy to give the wrong dose. It is helpful if the parents keep a notebook containing records of the baby's progress. Dates of immunisation, illnesses and appointments at the hospital should be noted. Certain other significant information will be useful, and the professionals concerned with the child's welfare can advise on what needs to be recorded. Items could range from a note of the day baby first grasped a toy to a chart of his bowel movements. Because of all the professional attention, many mothers of handicapped babies tend to become over-anxious about these matters. A child with a handicap is weighed, tested, probed and measured all his life, while a normal child is left to his own devices. Therefore a balance has to be struck, and it is not being suggested that parents should be wrapped in a lot of trivia. If the baby looks well, catches few colds, has a mottled skin and rounded limbs, it doesn't matter if he is not gaining weight very quickly.

The baby's mental health is as important as his general health. It is all too easy to provide for his physical needs and forget his psychological ones. As well as love and care, he needs the security of being in familiar surroundings, having the same methods used in handling him, and being given the opportunity to develop his own personality. He needs new experiences and plenty of attention. One of the worst punishments devised for a human being is that of sensory deprivation, that is of being shut alone in a sound-proof, featureless environment. The baby's first handicap is his disabling condition. It is easy for him to acquire a second handicap by being deprived of the experiences available to normal children.

Special Problems

A Baby with a Cleft Palate

Split lips and cleft palates occur in families from all races and all walks of life, and most of the children who are born with this condition are otherwise normal. The shock of seeing their baby's disfigured face can be very great for his parents and the rest of his family. Repair is a complicated business but the results are usually very good. Delicate and intricate surgery makes a dramatic improvement to the facial appearance, and the palate can be constructed in such a way as to provide reasonable function in speaking and feeding. As the child's teeth begin to grow, any dental defects which may appear can be dealt with adequately.

The most immediate problem for the baby with a cleft lip and/or a cleft palate is concerned with feeding. He has difficulty in sucking, which is normally performed by the tongue thrusting the nipple or teat against the roof of the mouth, the lips forming a seal. Often he learns to overcome this problem by making an adjustment of his tongue movements to compensate, but sometimes a small artificial palate is made which can be inserted in his mouth for feeding. The baby with a cleft palate may have some difficulty in swallowing, and sometimes this can cause him to regurgitate some of his food through his nose.

The baby's surgeon will always make every effort to ensure that the outward appearance of the mouth and lips is as normal as possible. The timing of operations varies according to the child's general condition and the surgeon's personal preference, and may take place within the first three months of the baby's life. Even the most grossly distorted little face will look surprisingly normal immediately following this operation. Further cosmetic surgery may be undertaken months or even years later if required.

Occasionally there can be hearing problems associated with a cleft palate, depending on the nature, location and severity of the condition, and many of these children have speech difficulties in the early stages of language development. However, a speech therapist can help both child and parents to overcome these so that the child is able to communicate freely.

A Baby with Congenital Dislocation of the Hips

About five babies in every thousand are born with instability in one or both hips. A clicking sound which can be detected when the baby's legs are moved through a certain range of movement, together with other signs, suggest to the doctor that the baby's hips could dislocate through poor formation of the joint.

The treatment is normally very simple, involving keeping the baby's hips immobile with the knees wide apart. This is done by putting a plastic, gutter-shaped splint on over the nappy and fastening it round the legs. The splint will be changed for larger ones as the baby grows, and it is important that it is worn all the time. When changing the nappy, the knees should be kept apart. Lifting the baby's bottom by holding both feet together, which will pull the knees together, should be avoided. The baby should be lifted by placing a hand under the base of the spine instead. The mother will soon get used to handling the baby in this splint. It will probably be found easy to carry him with his legs straddling the mother's hip, and if they are going out for a walk the baby will fit into a normal pram.

Almost all slings made for carrying babies hold them with their knees well apart, and are ideal for this baby. If the condition is not detected until the child is older, or if the splint has to be worn for several months, a few items of special equipment may be needed. At first it will be possible to feed the child on mother's lap, but as he grows bigger he could sit in a high chair with its sides cut away for meals and for short play periods. It is important to ensure that the child's trunk control is strong enough for him to sit up, and that he has been fastened to the chair securely. However, because the child's legs are not over the front of the seat, his weight will alter the centre of gravity of the chair, so he should not be left alone while he is in it. It is also advisable to fit wooden boards to the bottom of the chair legs, one each side, extending beyond the base of the chair by several inches at the front and at the back, like skis.

The baby can be laid on his stomach on the floor to strengthen neck, chest and arm muscles, and to play with toys. As he becomes stronger, he may enjoy lying on a small trolley and moving himself around the room. The trolley can be made of plywood, and should be T-shaped. It needs to be big enough to support him from chest to feet and well padded, and he should be fastened to it by one strap going round his chest and one on either side going round the top of each leg over his splint, so that he is safe. Three or four castors underneath will make the plat-form very easy to manoeuvre and prevent it from tipping, and if a cuff of stiff material such as rubber or leather is fixed round from the platform to the floor, toys, fingers and toes will not be caught underneath. All this equipment can be provided by the occupational therapist.

The baby will probably be able to discard his splints after a few months, although the doctor will still want to see him regularly to check on his progress until he has reached walking age or beyond.

A Baby with Osteogenesis Imperfecta

Osteogenesis imperfecta, or 'brittle bones', is a condition for which the cause is unknown. The degree of severity can vary considerably, from a child who appears to be only mildly affected to a baby who has suffered multiple fractures in the womb. Unfortunately, due to their weak structure and immature tissue, the child's bones not only break easily but also fail to repair adequately, so that bowing and shortening of the limbs is common.

The worst and most damaging time for the family of a child suffering from *osteogenesis imperfecta* is often during the first few months of the child's life, before this condition is diagnosed. The presentation at the doctor's surgery of a baby who is in pain, and the discovery of multiple fractures which were not present or not apparent at birth, often leads to the suspicion on that the injuries are not accidental. The extreme stress and feelings of anxiety which these suspicions cause to the baby's parents can be overwhelming, and can lead to breakdown. Add to this the hospitalisation of the baby which is sometimes necessary and the burden on the family may be intolerable. For these reasons, great sensitivity is necessary in approaching the parents of very young children with such injuries.

Unfortunately, even extreme care in handling a seriously affected child will not prevent fractures. However gentle his mother is, she may cause fractures very frequently. Her apprehension at handling her baby will inevitably cause tension in their relationship as the baby will pick up her anxiety. However, once she is taught how to handle her baby safely she will become more confident. She will need to be helped to realise that any fractures he may sustain are caused by his condition and not by her carelessness. She must come to terms with this if she is not to be overwhelmed by anxiety, and the rest of the family must also avoid any hint of criticism of the mother.

The Brittle Bones Society exists to support the families of children with *osteogenesis imperfecta*, and to provide information on progress in research and advice on the provision of aids.

A Baby with Talipes Equino-varus

Babies are sometimes born with one or both feet in an unusual position. If their ankles are too stiff for their feet to be pushed into a normal position, or the tiny joints inside their feet are so stiff that their feet are an unusual shape, then they need treatment immediately. The most common form of this condition is known as *talipes equino-varus* or TEV.

In many cases, the joints of the feet and ankles can be made more supple by means of exercises. The doctor or physiotherapist will demonstrate methods of stretching the muscle tendons of the baby's feet and ankles, and the parents should put the baby through the programme of exercises most conscientiously.

If the tendons are very tight, the doctor will probably encourage correct positioning by strapping the baby's feet and ankles, changing the strapping frequently, or by putting them in plaster. Occasionally, an operation may be necessary. Co-operation between the surgeon, physiotherapist and parents is vital in assisting to improve this condition, so that the baby is enabled to walk normally when the time comes. In every case, the doctor will wish to follow the child's progress by seeing him at intervals until he is quite sure that the child is able to walk without any trouble.

CHAPTER 2

A Handicapped Child and His Home

Very few homes have been designed with young children in mind, and very few parents will attempt to rear children in them without making some alterations. The amount of specialised equipment they add to the general furniture varies a little, but most families buy a cot, a pram, a high chair and a baby bath. Once the child has grown too big for these things he is expected to use adult furniture and equipment. Although he may be uncomfortable on the adult chair and be told frequently to sit still, sit upright and stop fidgeting, it is unlikely that he will be given any furniture scaled down to fit him. Most children manage to survive this stage in their lives without it affecting their physical development, largely because they do not stay in one position for any length of time. The physically handicapped child is much more at risk from ill-fitting furniture. Unable to wriggle, change his weight distribution, or get up and run off, he is likely to suffer all too easily from pins and needles, cramp and pressure sores. In extreme cases, he may develop deformities of the spine or limbs. Therefore it is essential that the equipment he uses is selected carefully, and is reviewed from time to time as he grows or his needs change. Children with no special physical problems are also at risk in some way or another in most homes. Parents are usually aware of the need to guard fires and to prevent children from tumbling down stairs, but it is often only when an accident occurs that they recognise other potential dangers.

While it is important to provide the child with an environment which takes his physical condition into account, the psychological requirements of a growing child should also be accommodated. He needs a pleasant, comfortable environment with plenty of people and toys around him, and he needs oportunities to explore that environment and its contents, to investigate, manipulate and negotiate and thereby to learn and develop.

Caring for a handicapped child can be tiring and time-consuming, so it is important to try to reduce the demands of household chores. Most mothers express anxieties about housekeeping standards, tidiness being a continuing problem. Investment in extra shelves and cupboards will mean that a lot of clutter can be kept off the floor and precious possessions out of reach. The child will then be more able to play in safety and without constant reminders to be careful or not to touch. If everything has its place, the child can be taught to find something, fetch it, and put it away without becoming confused; it cannot be stressed too highly that a blind or partially sighted child needs to know where everything is if he is to move around with any confidence. Thoughtful planning of the home environment can make life easier for the child, and rearrangement of storage and other furniture may well be worth the initial upheaval.

The Bedroom

If possible a handicapped child should have a room of his own. His needs may differ from those of the other children in the family, he may have special equipment which will take up too much space in a shared room, or he may disturb his room mate during the night. If a separate room is not available, then it may be possible to divide a shared room in some way — by standing a wardrobe at right angles to a wall or by hanging up a curtain — in order to give both occupants some privacy.

Unless the child is over-active, in which case his room needs to be sedative in effect, his room should be bright, cheerful and easy to clean. There are plenty of washable wallpapers in the shops and many curtain materials will withstand machine washing. It is no longer essential to use lino or vinyl on the floor if there are frequent spills, as some carpeting can now stand up to scrubbing. Loose rugs can be a danger to a child who is unsteady on his feet or to a mother carrying her child. Too many patterns can provoke restlessness and should be avoided, but a plain wall can be broken up with pictures, hung low enough for the child to enjoy them. The cheapest way of providing a change of pictures is to buy bright wrapping papers and fasten them up with one of the substances now available that does not damage walls or paintwork. If the child needs to keep a lot of equipment in his room, it will appear depressingly clinical unless an effort is made to keep the rest of the room attractive. Lighting should be bright enough to see to read a story or to attend to the child, but a dimmer-switch or a small lamp is invaluable if the parent has to go to him in the night. All forms of heating in the bedroom should be thermostatically controlled, with a safety cut-out which operates if the appliance is knocked over, and should not be hot to the touch.

Adequate storage space for the tidy organisation of clothes and toys will help the handicapped child to look after his belongings. There is no reason why the back of a door should sport only one hook, or why a single hook should carry only one item. The alternative is to hang up several draw-string bags to hold hairbrushes, socks, shoes or toys. Another possibility is for a panel of fabric with various pockets of different sizes sewn on it to be suspended from a length of dowelling. Peg board is sometimes used in kitchens or workshops to hang up tools, and often the shadow of the tool is painted on it. The same idea can be used in the bedroom or bathroom, with shadow spaces for comb, mirror and hairbrush or for toys. Storage boxes with padded tops make useful seats and help to accommodate more toys, and if the bed does not have drawers built in, drawers on castors to fit underneath it can be bought or made.

All windows are a potential hazard but those of an upper floor are particularly dangerous. There are various ways of preventing them from opening too far: casement windows can have restricting bars, and sash windows can have stops fixed in place. With a combined casement and transom window, the casement can be kept shut and only the transom used. This can be done permanently by removing all the hinges and fittings and screwing or nailing the casement in position. However, a simpler and less permanent method is merely to fasten a dome-headed screw down through one of the holes in the fixing bar, into the windowsill. If the window is low enough for the child to fall against it, a hard-wood crash barrier measuring about three inches by one inch can be fixed across the width of the window. This can be disguised by hanging a short net curtain from a wire on a level with the wood (see illustration). If this does not seem sufficient, or the child is likely to climb on to the windowsill, then whether or not the window opens, bars should be fastened over it. These must be vertical and should be not more than 2¾″/70 mm apart. It is possible to buy window bars which are ready-made and adjustable in size.

When purchasing a cot, there are certain features to look out for. The frame-work must be stable and well constructed and the depth should be over 26″/ 650 mm. Bars must be plain, parallel and vertical and there should be no pro-truding wooden or metal knobs or screws. The mattress must be thick enough not to slip under the rail, and the cot should be painted with non-toxic paint. Second-hand cots do not necessarily meet these requirements. There are now some folding cots on the market designed for camping and travelling. Although slightly smaller than the standard cot, they give more room than a pram or carry-cot and are convenient for holidays, but they must be erected with care. If the baby has been used to sleeping in a crib or carrycot, he may object to sleeping in a barred cot at first. It is a good idea to put him in his crib inside the big cot for several nights to get him used to the change of scene, before transferring him to sleeping in the cot.

There is no point in buying a short or 'junior' bed, since its length will limit its usefulness for the growing child. To prevent the child from wriggling down too far in a full-length bed, it can be made up apple-pie fashion. This also saves on laundry since it uses one sheet instead of two.

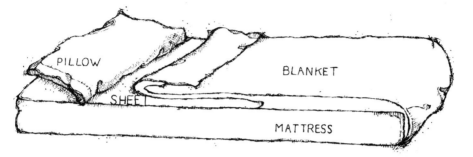

The child who needs a lot of nursing care in bed should sleep in a high bed to avoid back-strain in those who are looking after him. If he needs to get in and out of bed unaided, a small sturdy platform will provide him with a step. Since most modern beds are very low, it may be necessary to replace the legs with longer ones or to raise each leg on a block. If this is done the stability of the bed will have to be checked. If it takes two people to attend to the child's needs in bed, the bed should jut into the room leaving at least three feet each side of it for access, but if this is not the case, the bed can be placed in a corner to give more open space in the centre of the room.

Pillows must be firm but should not be used by a child under twelve months nor by an older child who has poor head control or limited head movement. It is desirable for bedding to be lightweight. A quilt will be easier for the child with limited strength to move under than will several tucked-in blankets. It may be useful to anchor it in some way to prevent its slipping off the bed, perhaps by using blanket clips. These are designed to fasten round the bars of a cot, but if they are to be used on a bed, suitable anchor points will have to be made. A child who kicks a great deal may be warmer in a sleeping bag, and a couple of washable ones can be used turn and turn about. Alternatively, if he is dressed warmly, for example in thermal underwear and a track suit, he will not need covers. For the immobile child it is important that he does not lie on rumpled bedding since he may become sore. Fitted sheets are less likely to crease and ruck than flat ones, and underblankets can be pulled taut at the corners of the bed with tapes. Sometimes it may be advised that the child should lie on a sheepskin or have a special ripple mattress, in order to assist in the prevention of pressure sores.

To protect the child from the danger of rolling out of bed, side rails can be attached to the headboard and footboard in a similar way as for a top bunk bed. However, if these are fixed permanently, daily bed-making may be a problem. Removable guard rails can be bought with arms that slide under the mattress, and the child's weight on these arms is usually sufficient to prevent the rails from slipping out.

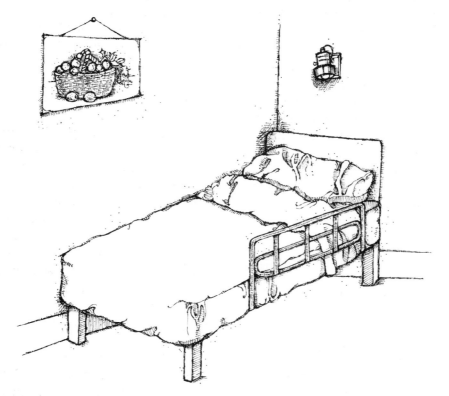

A baby-alarm is a useful investment for some families, but it might be worth considering the purchase of a two-way intercom instead. It will still serve as an alarm, but can also be used later on for older children or even installed elsewhere for the convenience of a different member of the family, for example between kitchen and workshed.

When planning a room for an older disabled child, it might be an advantage to install a small sink or vanity unit, perhaps even a refrigerator and a kettle, either to give him greater independence or to facilitate the work of caring for him. The effect of such special arrangements, however, should not be to confine him to his own room: he should always be included in the life of the rest of the family.

One final point to note is that no drugs or medicine should ever be stored or left in a child's room.

The Living Room

The normal family living room is not used just for living in but also for housing
some precious possessions, many of which are rather vulnerable. The need to
display such things is important in creating the required atmosphere, and instead
of locking their favourite things away, many parents compromise by putting
them out of reach. The best solution is to make a narrow plate shelf right round
the room at a fairly high level, as seen in old-fashioned tea rooms. This will not
only hold plates but other china, vases, ornament, plants and small books. If
cupboards cannot be locked, small hands can be kept out of them effectively by
fastening the knobs together with elastic bands or garters. Where the knobs are
too far apart for this, elasticated luggage-retaining cords, sold in various lengths,
can be used. There is also a special drawer-catch on the market which restricts
the opening of drawers but can be quickly and simply released. Avoiding
possible damage in this way makes it easier for the parents to concentrate on
such social training as respect for possessions. The child should also be taught
not to jump on the furniture or pick the curtains or wallpaper. This cannot be
done effectively in an atmosphere of constant admonition, but it is essential if
the parents are to visit other people's homes with some confidence in the handicapped child's behaviour. If the child cannot be allowed in the living room
without supervision, then a lock can be fitted to the door or a bolt fastened on
the outside of it, well out of reach. The same can be done for other rooms, of
course, especially those containing potential dangers like the kitchen.

Since many children learn to walk by clinging to the living room furniture, it is
important to ensure that they cannot harm themselves by doing this. All tall
furniture, such as cupboards or bookcases, should be fastened securely to the
wall near the top so that there is no possibility of pulling them over. Some
smaller items, chests of drawers or hi-fi cupboards, may tip when grasped so it is
wise to fasten these also, and television sets and record players on spindly legs
can be remounted on stouter legs, fastened to the top of a small table, or fixed to
the wall on shelf brackets. If the arms of armchairs are set outside the line of the
legs, the chances are that they will tip if leant over or if pulled on from below.
This can be tested by putting weight on one arm when no one is sitting in the
chair. If it tips up, it is a danger to a child with poor mobility who will use every
piece of furniture as a hand hold. This might mean putting it in a room the child
does not use or wedging it tightly between other furniture so that it cannot tip.
Similarly, many chairs and settees will tip over backwards all too easily, and
these must be dealt with in the same way. If the child falls when trying to stand
against a piece of furniture, he is likely to bang his chin or forehead. To prevent
him from hurting himself too seriously, it may be necessary to round off the
corners of shelves, coffee tables and any wooden arms of chairs with sandpaper
or a plane. All these points should be taken into consideration when shopping
for new furniture. Unfortunately, many handicapped children cannot save
themselves in the way that a normal child can, but he must learn to take some

knocks. Over-protection at this stage will lead to anxiety and timidity when facing situations in the future outside the home.

Apart from those problems that affect the furniture, there are various other safety points to consider in the living room. The major hazard is the fire, whether it be solid fuel, gas or electric. It needs to be enclosed by an extendable guard which will encompass the hearth and fasten to the wall each side of the fireplace. In the case of an open solid fuel fire, a fine-mesh spark guard within this is also desirable.

Electrical flexes should be fastened to the wall, using insulated staples or cable clips. They should never be longer than necessary, although they must not be stretched. In order to prevent the need for them to lie across the floor, all electrical equipment should as far as possible be placed against the wall. It may be necessary to have additional sockets installed. Sockets can be bought with indicator bulbs that light up when the socket is switched on, and socket covers are available to prevent plugs from being pulled out or fingers and small items from being poked into the holes. The latter can also be guarded against by inserting a dummy plug when the socket is not in use.

Loose mats and rugs are a danger anywhere in the home, to all members of the family. The child who walks with difficulty, with or without walking aids, and the child who propels his own wheelchair, should never be expected to negotiate these obstacles, nor should an adult carrying a child in her arms. Rugs are normally used to save the carpet from wear, but it is far more important to save the family from falls.

The small baby and the child with little or no mobility spend a lot of their time in the living room as spectators. They need to be able to see not only the television set but what the rest of the family is doing and also what is going on outside. If he cannot move, or even turn his head, without help, the child's position must be changed frequently for him. This is important not only to enable him to observe but also to prevent him from becoming stiff or uncomfortable in one position. It is a useful experiment for parents to place themselves where the child normally sits, with their heads on the same level as his. What can be seen, heard, felt or touched from this position? If he were turned to the right or left, laid down flatter or propped up straighter, would he be able to see or feel more? Above all, is he able to see and hear other members of the family? Very often a simple rearrangement of furniture will make a big difference to the quality of the child's experiences, and moving his chair from one part of the room to another gives him more variety and novelty. He may enjoy looking at a bird table in the back garden, watching television, being placed near the front window when children are coming out of school, watching his mother knit or use the sewing machine, and looking out for the arrival of his father's car. If he cannot get to something which interests him it can be placed nearer his chair; and if it is impossible for him to see people in the street directly, a mirror can be positioned in such a way that he can see them through it.

It is important not to have the radio or record player on for too long, as the constant sound will tend to mask other noises. It will be more interesting for him to hear and learn to identify such sounds as approaching footsteps, the laughter of children, the noise of a lorry and the hum of the refrigerator. The aim should be always to help him to develop whatever abilities he has as he may be able to employ them later in compensation for those he cannot utilise.

The Dining Room

Joining the family when all the members are gathered together for a meal is interesting and stimulating for the young child. A small baby needs a high seat so that he can watch what is going on, but it will have to be tilted back so that his head has some support. As he gains more control of his head, he can be tilted into a more upright sitting position so that he can see more around him. While he is very small, a roll of soft material each side of his body, extending from the top of his head to his buttocks, will stop him from slumping sideways in the seat and protect his head from bumps if his neck muscles get tired. As he grows bigger and fills out the seat more, these rolls can be discarded. However, he must always wear a harness when he is not lying completely flat.

The type of harness the child wears will depend a little on what body control he has. He must wear a waist strap which should be not less than two inches wide or it will be uncomfortable, and a crutch strap so that he does not slide down. Children who have a tendency to cross their legs will benefit from a padded pommel which can be used instead of the crutch strap, but it must be deep enough to prevent the child from crossing his legs over the top of it. Some children will also need to have shoulder straps to prevent them from slumping forward. These should be fastened to the waist strap and either cross each other on the chest, which makes them a bit awkward to put on, or fasten together to the centre of the chair behind the neck. If they rise vertically and fasten separately, the child can slip forward between them.

As the child grows it is very important that the furniture he uses fits him. Adults can test this for themselves by sitting on a backless bar stool for several minutes, allowing their feet to dangle. In time they will begin to experience backache, their thighs will start to shake, pressure will be felt just above the backs of the knees, and pins and needles may develop in the feet.

Then they should try sitting on a bed pushed against the wall. At first, they should sit upright with both feet on the floor and nothing to support the back. Then they should lean back, so that both shoulders are resting on the wall, still without any cushions. Finally, they should move back until they are sitting with the back flat against the wall and both legs stuck straight out in front. These are the postures all children are compelled to adopt by sitting on furniture designed for adults. However, a normal child does not sit still for long and is able to wriggle or get up when he becomes too uncomfortable. The handicapped child may not have the initiative or the ability to do either. For him, scaled-down

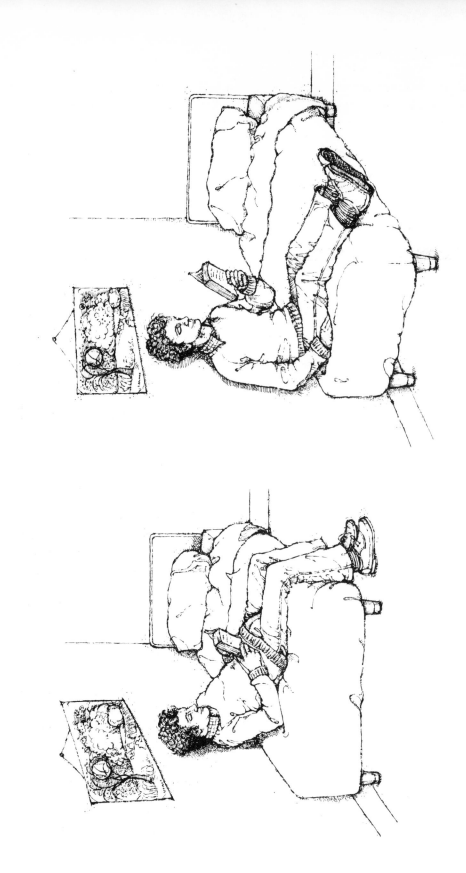

furniture, designed to meet any special needs he may have, is essential.

In order to be comfortable and promote good posture, a chair should fit the child in certain ways. The width is important, since the sides of the chair should hold his legs parallel to each other. If this is too narrow, there will be pressure on

the hips, and if it is too wide the floppy child will be able to splay his legs and allow his hip ligaments to slacken. The length of the seat from front to back is also crucial. The whole of the child's thighs should be supported while he is sitting. With his buttocks as far back in the chair as possible, the front of the seat should come to just behind his knees. A footrest is vital and it should be located so that he can put his feet down flat on it. If the foot rest is too high, the backs of his thighs will be pushed off the seat. If it is too low, the weight of his legs will pull his thighs down hard against the seat and he will experience pressure and possibly pins and needles in his legs. Since many children's limbs seem to grow longer suddenly, the height of the footrest should be checked frequently. The back of the chair should extend above the child's head to give him support when he gets tired, or have a removable extension so that he can be taught head control, and the length of time during which his head is unsupported can be increased gradually. Armrests should be low enough for him to sit with his elbows on them and his upper arms vertical without his shoulders being hunched up. The chair must be stable, and harness should be provided in the same way as for the small baby. Aim always for the child to be sitting symmetrically with his back flat against the backrest, his knees and feet together, and both arms forward to the same degree.

Once the child is sitting in a chair that fits him, the next objective is to find the right tray or table for him. It should be positioned at the same height as the armrests and should always remain horizontal, regardless of the angle at which his chair is tilted. A large tray which extends round the sides of the chair, or a table with a semi-circular cut-out the width of the child's seat, is ideal. It will give him extra support for his arms beyond the width of the chair and extra surface on which to play with his toys. Again, stability is essential. Adults can try the effects of eating from a high or low table themselves, by sitting at a normal table on a high bar stool or on a low footstool. The high seat will cause backache, and the low one will make the arms ache. There is no point in giving the child more problems than he has already: everything should be done to help him overcome his difficulties.

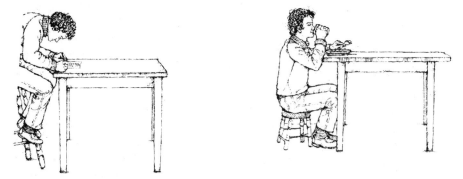

One good seat that fits the child can be used as a high chair, reclining seat or car seat, but it is necessary to ensure that it does all these jobs efficiently. If this is not the case, separate seats should be used for different functions. If the child is misshapen in a particular way, he can best be accommodated in a seat which has been moulded to his body contours. This can usually be done at the local hospital. The physiotherapist supports the child in his optimum position while the staff of the plaster room take a cast of his body. The staff of the occupational therapy department should then be able to arrange for the making of one or several moulded seats to fit the child. These can be adapted for use in a wheel-chair, car or bath.

Once the child has an adequate seat, it is all too easy for it to become his prison — something he is fastened into in the morning and taken out of in the evening. He must be given frequent changes of position and scenery and opportunities to learn to move about. The physiotherapist should be asked to suggest a timetable for this as the needs of all handicapped children vary.

The Kitchen

The kitchen is both the most interesting and the most dangerous place for a child to enter. With cupboards and drawers full of potential toys, from wooden spoons and pudding basins to brightly coloured packets, the opportunities it offers for play and experiment are immense. Saucepan lids need not be used only as lids for saucepans: they make effective cymbals, shields, breast-plates and spinning tops, and can also be employed to draw round when making pictures. With a bowl of water and a selection of jugs, sieves, funnels and pots, a child will not only play happily for some time but will discover a lot about volume and elementary mechanics. By allocating him a cupboard or box of his own containing kitchen utensils that cannot be damaged or be harmful to him, he may be prevented from touching the rest of the cookery equipment. However, if a child is going to be allowed into the kitchen to enjoy such delights, he must be protected from danger. Worktops with jutting corners can be made safer by adding a rounded piece of chipboard not less than three-quarters of an inch thick to the corner, fixing it with a small L-shaped bracket. Corners of tables should also be rounded off, and if this proves difficult they should be padded. One way of doing this is by making a fitted tablecloth with elastic or drawstrings in the hem, and sewing the padding on the inside of it. Apart from this type of fitted padded cloth, no tablecloths should ever be used: if the child pulls at one he can bring things over on to himself.

When the cooker is not in use it should be turned off at a remote switch so that no amount of knob-twiddling can turn it on. It is preferable for all controls to be at the back of the cooker when there are young children in the kitchen, though this does mean that the cook has to stretch her arm and hand over heat and steam in order to adjust them, which has its dangers. Unfortunately some safety measures can mean inconvenience for adults: for example, pan handles should always be turned away from the front of the cooker, but they may then become uncomfortably hot and should be held cautiously. Similarly, a cooker guard which surrounds the hob will safeguard children from spills during cooking but means that the cook has to lift the pan over the guard rather than slide it on to the worktop when the contents are cooked. Clothes should never be aired over the cooker, or aprons, teacloths and curtains hung near it. Matches, spills and tapers should be kept well out of reach.

Electrical appliances should be placed at the back of the worktop, as close to the socket as possible, and their flexes must be short. For example, it should not be necessary for a kettle to have more than about three feet of cable. All sockets should be switched, not live, and adaptors to take several plugs should not be used. It is a good idea to seal over the switch which serves the freezer with a piece of sticky tape. This will prevent it from being switched off accidentally, but the tape can be removed fairly easily when necessary. Many accidents happen during ironing; not only is there a risk of burns, but an iron is also quite heavy. The ironing board needs to be very stable, or to be hooked to the wall or worktop in order to steady it, so that there is no risk of its toppling over or of the iron being wobbled off. A flex holder will prevent the flex from dangling, so that it won't tempt small fingers. Needless to say, a child should never be left alone in a room with an iron on an ironing board, but it is also risky for him to play near it while his mother is ironing in case she drops the iron or he trips her up. Scissors, knives and other sharp gadgets should be kept locked away, and so should all plastic bags and sealing material: these are deadly toys.

Most adults recognise these as elementary precautions, but they cannot be reiterated too often in the case of handicapped children who are vulnerable through their disabilities or their slow development for much longer than the normal child.

If the kitchen cannot be made safe enough, it may be worth trying to put the child in a playpen while he is in there, provided there is sufficient space. There is nothing wrong with using a playpen for short periods, and the child will not object if he gets used to it gradually from an early age. He should not be put in it for punishment, however, as he will then react very badly to being put in it at all times, and he should not be allowed to become bored in it. In the long run it may be easier, especially with a small kitchen, to keep the child right out of it. If there is an adjacent room which can be child-proofed, he can be confined to that yet be in close touch if the door is left open and a safety gate fitted across it. Perhaps it may be possible to cut the kitchen door in two to make a stable door, so that the child can watch his mother while she is busy. Even if the kitchen is reasonably safe, and is clean and comfortable, it is not the nicest place for the mother and child to spend a lot of time in. Many chores can be done in a different room. Ironing, for example, can be done anywhere in the house except the bathroom, and provided the furniture and floor covering are protected, even messy jobs like preparing vegetables or cleaning shoes can be done in another room.

The Bathroom

It is a pity that the average bathroom is so small, as it has to accommodate a great deal of activity. If the lavatory is in a separate room it has the advantage of being accessible while the bathroom is in use, but the bathroom which contains a lavatory is usually a good deal larger than one that does not. Whatever its size, the bathroom can be a dangerous place. The rules governing the use of electricity in the bathroom are clear cut, but unfortunately they have only been introduced recently so if the house is of the older type, steps should be taken to check that it conforms to all the modern standards.

It is not essential to have a lock on the bathroom door but if one is used it should be fitted high up on the door above child's reach, or a two-way lock which can be opened from the outside if necessary, should be installed. Good practice by the family as a whole helps to teach and safeguard the special child. Thus if every member of the family uses a rubber mat inside the bath to guard against slipping, and a similar mat of non-slip material beside the bath for stepping out, a great many accidents caused by slipping on a wet surface can be avoided.

The other chief cause of accidents in the bathroom is hot water. Many children are badly scalded every year, and although most of these scalds occur in the kitchen, a great many happen in the bathroom. Some cold water should always be run into the bath or wash-basin first, and an adult should be present when the child gets into the bath. The water heating thermostat should not be set too high — 130°F/54°C is sufficient. All cleaning materials should be locked away after use.

The child can be encouraged to understand his own identity by using his own flannel, towel and toothbrush. It is a good idea to colour-code these articles for each member of the family as it will assist the handicapped child in recognising his own. He can also hang up his things in the correct place after use, provided this is in a position that is easy for him to reach. There should also be a mirror fixed at a suitable height for the child, to assist his independence in keeping himself clean and tidy.

There are several aids which the handicapped child can use to make him independent in the lavatory, for example a sturdy platform, grab rails or a support such as the Mechanaids Toilet Aid (see illustration on p. 76). However, long before he reaches that stage he should be getting used to being in the lavatory. A start can be made using his potty in the lavatory if there is enough space, or if there is not, he should sit on it in the bathroom. The potty should be strong, rigid and large. The majority of potties are far too small, so that by the time the child is old enough to understand what a potty is for, he is too big to sit on it in comfort. It is very difficult for small children to use the lavatory without help, but holding a child over the pan is quite awkward and tiring. Mothercare currently manufactures a trainer seat which clips on to a standard lavatory seat and reduces its size. Cindico also makes a trainer seat which has a back and a harness. The Crossland toilet seat stands over the lavatory and gives maximum support. It should not be used for any other purpose, or the child will become confused.

In and Out of Doors

For the child who is in a wheelchair, or using sticks, crutches or a walking frame, the width of doorways is crucial. These should be not less than 2′3″/680 mm wide and there should not be any furniture obstructing the approach from either side. Sills and thresholds should be removed, and sliding doors must be suspended from a high track and not floor mounted. Doors which can be pushed open from either direction to swing two ways are easy to manage but rather impractical in the average home, so sliding doors are the best option for the disabled child. All doors leading outside should be lockable.

Staircases should have a safety gate permanently fixed at both top and bottom when there are young children about the house, and in the home of the older child who is unsteady on his feet. This is not over-protection but is a sensible precaution since a child can be seriously injured by falling down stairs. It is advisable to install gates which are hinged and can be fastened securely, rather than the loose, removable type, and the bars of a sturdy old cot may be suitable for this. There should be no horizontal bars in these gates, for it must not be possible to clamber over them. If the stairs are composed of treads with open risers, these must be boarded in, at least temporarily, as must open banister rails if they are set too wide apart. Hand rails are usually too high to give any support to a small child so it is sensible to add a rail set much lower down, preferably one on each side of the staircase. These can easily be raised as the child grows. Lighting on the staircase must be bright and capable of being operated from the top or bottom, and a nightlight is useful on the landing. Nothing must ever be left on the stairs.

It may be necessary to re-plan the hallway in order to accommodate a pram, pushchair or wheelchair. Alternatively, it may be possible to house these under the stairs or in a garage or shed. In the latter case, bedding should not be left outside as it will get damp, but stored indoors. If the older child is expected to take care of his clothes, he will need a coat-hook which he can reach unaided and somewhere for him to put hat, gloves and shoes.

The garden or back yard is the place where the child gets most of his fresh air, but he must be able to play there in safety. To prevent him from straying on to the road it must be ensured that walls, fences and gates are high enough and fastened securely. Hawthorn, holly and sweet briar can make impenetrable hedges eventually, but take a long time to grow to that stage. A garden pond will have to be filled in, for a time at any rate, and so will streams and ditches. A rockery sited near a wall may enable a child to climb out of the garden. However, a great many of the skills required for balance and co-ordination are learnt in the space which a garden affords, and the traditional toys like swings, tricycles and climbing frames will facilitate this. Unfortunately, as the child grows in confidence, potential hazards increase. If the mother can arrange to do some of her chores outside, she can give some supervision.

Major Changes to the Home

If the child is severely handicapped, more equipment to care for him will become necessary as he grows bigger. While it may be fairly easy for parents to carry a small child up and down stairs, and to lift him on and off the lavatory and in and out of the bath, some mechanical help will be needed as he becomes heavier. A stair-lift may be required to enable him to reach his bedroom and the bathroom, and a bath hoist may need to be installed. If the staircase is too narrow or the bathroom too small for such additions, radical re-planning may be the only answer.

The first and most simple way of altering a home to give more space to a handicapped person is to change the use of some rooms. If there are two rooms downstairs, one could be converted into his bedroom, and an upstairs room used as a study, playroom or extra living room. If a downstairs bathroom is needed, perhaps part of the kitchen could be altered. It is essential that the handicapped child lives downstairs as he grows older. A conservatory or garage could be converted into a bedroom and bathroom for him, or perhaps an extra room built on somewhere. If there are other children in the family, a loft conversion may give them more space and prevent them from feeling crowded out by the needs of their handicapped sibling.

Before embarking on changes of any kind, the child's long-term prospects must be considered:

(1) Is he likely to get worse, and need more space for aids?
(2) Is his condition likely to improve, and require less equipment?
(3) Will he always live at home, or may he go away to boarding school or residential care?
(4) Will work keep the family in the area, or is a move to another part of the country likely within a few years?

If the answers to these questions are in doubt then major changes should be avoided until the future becomes clearer.

Structural alterations and additions can be very expensive, and so can moving house. Although the family may qualify for some financial assistance, the following possibilities should be explored before undertaking such changes:

(1) Can the use of any rooms be altered?
(2) Would some simple change, like the addition of a wash-basin to one room, go some way towards solving the problems?
(3) Can use be made of existing space in any way, by converting the loft or garage for example?
(4) Could a pantry, a walk-in cupboard or the space under the stairs be converted into an extra lavatory or shower, and if so would it help?

Before any work is begun, it is important to ascertain what financial aid will be forthcoming. Most agencies are unable to contribute to work which is already in hand or actually completed. The source of this help often depends on the alterations being considered: parents need detailed guidance in this respect, and a social worker may be able to advise on which agencies to approach.

If moving house appears to be the best way of meeting the requirements, a checklist of needs, not only of the handicapped child but also of other members of the family, should be carefully compiled. It will be different in each case but might include such things as the following:

(1) Is the new house within reasonable reach of the child's school and those of the other children in the family?
(2) Is it also a reasonable distance from the child's hospital or clinic?
(3) Is the garden big enough for the child to enjoy?
(4) Are shops and other facilities close at hand?
(5) Is it a long way to commute to work each day?
(6) Can supporting friends and relatives still visit as often as before?

These are just a few of the points to be considered. Since moving house is such a complicated business, it needs to offer substantial advantages. It is often easier to adapt the present family home, bearing in mind that although responsibility for the handicapped child is likely to be a long-term one, other children will in the normal course of things become independent and move away.

CHAPTER 3

A Child With a Physical Handicap

The needs of a physically handicapped child as a person are all too easily made secondary to the more conspicuous needs of his handicap. He may be subjected to hours of mindless and repetitive exercises, and his right to privacy and dignity in the bathroom and lavatory may be forgotten when dealing with his functional requirements. His condition may be discussed in front of him as if he were a clinical object instead of a sensitive personality with the same emotions as any other child. The attitude and handling of those who deal with him will determine to a considerable extent the view the child has of himself. If his carers are calm, sensible and discreet he will accept his problems in the same way, neither making a fuss nor pretending there is nothing wrong. However, if they are aggressive and resentful he will come to hate his handicap and make life difficult for everyone who tries to help him.

For parents a major problem is to give the child the care he needs without spoiling him. The time will come, at school, in hospital or in the community, when he is not the most important person around, and if his wishes have been gratified and the world has revolved round him up till then, he will feel let down and adjustment to the new situation will be very hard. The greatest gift parents and teachers can give the physically handicapped child is his own independence, because it is only through personal independence that he can lead a fully normal life. To give him this, it is necessary to allow him to struggle to accomplish tasks of which he is capable without helping him. As soon as he can hold his head up, he must spend increasing time with his head unsupported, and from the day he first manages to take his own socks off, his parents will know he is quite capable of doing this for himself. But learning to be independent is a lengthy process for any child, and it takes a great deal of practice to become quick and skilful. The child should be given plenty of time and plenty of opportunity, and help should be offered if the child is obviously tired or unwell. However hard he tries to be independent, it may be many years before the child is able to do everything without help, therefore he needs to be taught how to ask for assistance politely, to accept it gracefully, and to thank people for their help. It is also important to teach him how to decline help in a considerate manner if it has been offered unnecessarily. He must learn to appreciate how much he may have to depend on the goodwill of others from time to time.

Mobility

Physically handicapped children must be handled slowly and carefully, but firmly. They should be approached from the front so as not to startle them, and told what is about to happen. The child should be lifted by placing both hands around his ribs immediately under the armpits, and not by gripping him round the top of his arms, and then brought slowly up. He should not be swung around or moved quickly as he will become confused and disorientated. He should be supported firmly, as if he is held gently he will feel insecure. The only child who should be handled with caution is the child suffering from *osteogenesis imperfecta*, as described in Chapter 1. All others need plenty of handling, cuddling and general movement in order to become aware of their bodies. An adult does not have to think about the position of his body nor of how to set about making a movement, but he had to learn these things as a child by a process of trial and error and repeated practice, gradually achieving awareness of the machinery which worked his body. For the less active child, these movements have to be made for him until he can practise for himself.

If he is left lying in bed, the handicapped child will be unable to see much of what is happening around him, and because his movement is limited he will have no way of making anything happen. To some extent he will have to be taught how to play and play materials will have to be brought to him. From an early age the child should be placed on his stomach on the floor for short periods, to help him to want to lift his head, to roll and to make the swimming movements which are a forerunner of crawling. He should be encouraged to bend and stretch, and pushed to make him roll over. If he is very late in starting to crawl, he will probably benefit from a low trolley designed to support his body off the floor so that he can achieve mobility by paddling movements of his hands and feet. Alternatively, he can be held up by using a towel as a sling to support him from armpits to hips.

Some children never crawl but get along by means of shuffling on their bottoms, and some do neither but pull themselves up to standing and walking without ever moving along the floor. However, all children need a reason for moving and their motivation is usually to reach a goal such as a person or toy, or even food and drink. For example, a balloon suspended near him will encourage him to reach out and it will also respond to him by moving. The most responsive plaything a child can have, however, is another person, and when one person cannot give him time and attention, someone else can be drawn in to participate in the fun and games.

Once he has mobility of his own, he can be presented with toys which roll away. These will encourage him to try and move after them although it is important not to allow him to become too frustrated in his attempts to attain a desired toy. If they are too far away he will give up, too near and he will stretch for them without having to move. It is at this time that the handicapped child may find a quick and easy way of doing something, a trick or a knack. However, it may not be of use to him when he is grown up, or it may be actually encouraging the development of a permanent deformity. If the physiotherapist considers this to be the case, she will advise on the correct method for him to use, and may also recommend certain exercises, positions and movement patterns to be employed. Such recommendations should be carried out according to instructions, especially with regard to frequency and duration, as the child can be over-tired from too much or become too stiff from too little exercise.

Aids to Mobility

If the child needs to wear special shoes, splints or calipers, it is necessary to be clear how often and in what circumstances they should be on or off, and to use them accordingly. Some splints are termed 'rest splints' and are commonly worn at night, others may need to be worn continuously, day and night. One child may need to be encouraged to walk indoors with bare feet, or to be kept in special shoes throughout his waking hours; another may need to wear calipers all the time, or only when he is practising walking. Such advice is very important but needs to be tempered by keeping a watchful eye on the child. If he dislikes his aids in spite of calm use of them, or if he is developing any kind of sores from their use, then the matter should be referred back immediately to the doctor or consultant for further guidance.

The child may need to use sticks, crutches or a walking frame in order to be mobile, and will be assessed for them by the physiotherapist. These are part of his independence and more useful to him than such supports as holding on to his mother or father or a convenient piece of furniture. Since he cannot take his parents or pieces of furniture with him wherever he goes for the rest of his life, so he must learn to use his aids. All mobility aids, however, can be 'dressed up' so that they will be more fun to use; in a very real sense they must become a part of the child's life, never to be left behind. Wheelchairs are obtainable through an

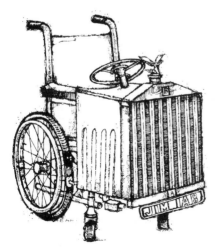
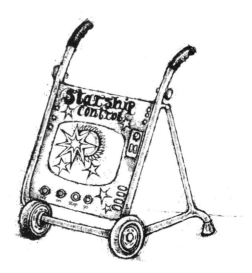

occupational therapist. If the child has a wheelchair he should be encouraged to propel it himself. At home it may be necessary to rearrange the furniture to give him more space to manoeuvre, but it is a small price to pay for his being able to come and go as he pleases and to fetch and carry things for himself. This piece of equipment lends itself to conversion into a variety of different vehicles that will make the child the envy of his friends, and the addition of badges and flags and even a horn or bell if the family can stand it, will make it still more attractive.

A child who uses mobility aids may tend to wear out certain parts of his clothing rather fast. Although it is possible for parents to obtain financial help with clothing if their child does wear things out very quickly (the social worker will be able to provide details of this), the wide range of sources of secondhand clothing will often meet most day-to-day needs and the current fashion climate of frayed hems and colourful patches is a boon.

Incontinence

Whatever the reason for a child's inability to control his bladder or bowel, the problems of management are basically the same. No child should have to suffer the embarrassment of a wet and smelly life, so regular care is essential. It is a mistake to restrict the child's drinking in the belief that this will make for easier control. He must have a high fluid intake to avoid developing kidney disorders, and his bladder should be emptied every two hours. Control comes partly through habit. The child can be taught how to empty his bladder manually if necessary, by putting his clenched fist on his tummy just below the navel and pressing down towards the middle of his pelvis. If constipation is a problem, advice can be sought from the health visitor or hospital; many physically handicapped children use suppositories successfully. Until he has achieved control he should be kept in nappies or special incontinence pads, such as Kanga pads which fit into special pants, and he should be changed as soon as he is wet or dirty. Care must be taken to keep him clean and free from sores, and he has to be taught the importance of this himself. Some children may know when they want to use the lavatory but be unable to communicate this, and some children know and start heading in the right direction but are unable to reach the lavatory in time. Finding some way for the child to signal his need is worth a good deal of trouble — as is making it easier for him to get to the lavatory. For the child who is not aware of his need, one of the many alarm systems on the market can be tried.

The one thing that all these children need is a regular routine in order to manage their problems. A basic pattern is to give the child the opportunity to use the lavatory when he wakes up, after each meal, before he goes out and before he goes to bed, and at least every two hours between these times. It soon becomes a normal and accepted part of life, causing no special fuss. The child should be taught to care for himself as much and as soon as possible, but supervision should be maintained, in particular at night, to ensure that his skin is clean and dry.

The other people with whom he spends his time should know how to manage the child's incontinence, to avoid embarrassing him and upsetting them, and when he goes out a change of clothes and the necessary cleaning materials should go with him.

Going Into Hospital

It is inevitable that most children are going to need to visit hospital at some time in their lives, and a few of them may need to stay as an in-patient for a while. In order to reduce some of the anxiety that this may cause, the child should be familiarised with the idea of hospitals. There are two excellent books for children on the subject: *Miffy in Hospital* by Dick Bruna for the young ones, and *Paul in Hospital* by Camilla Jessel for the older ones, both published by Methuen. Reading these and discussing them together as well as playing such games as 'Dolls' Hospital' will help to pave the way. It is also possible to visit some of the larger hospitals simply as an outing. If there is a snack bar in the Out-patients Department the child might enjoy having something pleasant to eat and drink whilst watching nurses in uniform and people in white coats going by. He

could also be introduced to the hospital lift, especially if he is unused to the sensation of going up or down in one, useful preparation for a future stay in hospital. At home, the child can be encouraged to play at hospitals, with well-bandaged teddies as patients.

When the child is admitted to hospital, it is highly desirable that his mother should go with him and stay with him. The rest of the family will be able to manage without her more easily than he will, provided they remain in their own familiar surroundings. They should not be sent to stay in the homes of other relatives or friends, unless they are in habit of doing so, or they may feel as insecure as the hospitalised child. Most hospitals today recognise the need for a mother to stay with her child but sometimes it is necessary for the parents to negotiate for this. Hospitals are busy places and it is easy for parents to feel hesitant about sitting with their child or moving about the ward for fear of upsetting the staff, but their role is as essential as the medical and nursing care. The rest of the family should be encouraged to visit the child frequently to maintain contact with him. When he is discharged from hospital, he will derive great comfort from being back in the security of his own familiar room, and it is important for it to look the same as it did when he left it. This is not the time to redecorate it or to change the carpet, curtains or furniture since he may not settle so well when he returns and he may dread having to go away again for fear of being ousted altogether.

Caring for a Sick Child at Home

If it is essential for a child to stay in bed, the guiding principle is to make this as pleasant and easy as possible for him and for those who are caring for him. The bed should be placed near a window so that he can see outside, but the window must be securely fastened, barred if necessary, and free of draughts. If this is not possible or the child cannot move, a mirror can be positioned temporarily in such a way that he can see more through the window or so that he can see who is coming through the door without having to crane his neck. It is useful to have a table or a tray on legs over the bed, and to give the child plenty of very simple things to do which will not make a mess. A sick child will prefer not to attempt to do anything which is very demanding. There needs to be a comfortable chair in the room for whoever is caring for him or visiting him, and the radio or tape recorder can be transferred from the living room to give both child and 'nurse' something to listen to. The room should be kept clean and attractive, and use of an air-freshener will modify the sick-room atmosphere. How much attention the child needs depends on his personality, but a quiet companion is always appreciated.

As soon as possible he should be brought down to the living room. He can lie on a comfortable settee or camp bed during the day, perhaps moving to a hammock, sag-bag or air-bed for a change of position, dressed warmly in soft clothing, and zipped into a sleeping bag to keep out draughts. He will feel less isolated once he is downstairs and it will save his family from frequent journeys up and down. It will also mean that his mother can catch up with some of the chores while still keeping an eye on him, and the family as a whole will be together once more.

Caring for the handicapped child when he is unwell is a time when extra effort is needed and will mean giving him more attention than usual. He will be less able to amuse himself, through weakness and apathy, and will appreciate someone reading to him and keeping him company far more than any new toy. It is one of the times when things like housework have to go by the board.

Common Handicapping Conditions

Whilst many special needs are general across a range of physical handicaps, particular conditions have specific characteristics which have to be taken into account in management and treatment. It is also necessary to have insight into the nature of the handicap: for a parent this may mean becoming something of a specialist in their own child's disability, including joining the relevant association concerned to support the families of children who have the same condition.

A Child with Cerebral Palsy

Children with cerebral palsy may be spastic, flaccid, athetoid or ataxic* in one or more limbs or their entire body, and their intelligence range is from normal to severely subnormal. Some of them may also suffer from the additional problems of visual or auditory impairment, and may have difficulties with speech. Therefore any generalised description, or suggestions for management, can only be used as a guide and must be interpreted according to the condition of each individual child.

It is very important for all children with cerebral palsy that their parents should be given the advice at the earliest possible opportunity because careful handling, positioning and exercise will help the child to develop and will also play a considerable role in the prevention of deformity. It should be explained that unequal strength of groups of muscles may cause joints to acquire an abnormal range of movement or to stiffen into an increasingly unnatural position. Treatment of any kind by a therapist can only be administered at specific times and for limited periods, and because of these constraints it cannot be effective in isolation. It is largely up to the parents, who are with the child constantly, to carry out the exercises which the therapist has shown them and to ensure that

---

* Athetosis is a condition in which there is an almost continuous alternation of extension and relaxation of the limbs, particularly of the hands and fingers; the movements are slow and involuntary. Ataxia is primarily a problem in the co-ordination of voluntary movement. Both are forms of cerebral palsy.

the child is positioned in the optimum way when he is at rest or when he is performing an activity. They should also adhere as far as possible to the suggested
frequency and duration of the exercise periods; if the period is reduced it may
be ineffectual, and if it is increased the child may suffer from fatigue. Exercise
will usually take the form of moving all joints through the normal range several
times a day, and positioning will normally be in symmetry and in such a way as
to encourage control of head, trunk and limbs and to discourage abnormal
reflexes.

One of the most noticeable physical characteristics of many children with
cerebral palsy is their bodily over-reaction to certain stimuli. For example, most
young children, when spoken to, will blink and attempt to turn or raise the head
but many children with cerebral palsy will assume the 'Moro' reaction — both
head and arms flying up and back. It is because of this over-reaction that such
items of nursery equipment as 'baby-bouncers' should not be used. They
encourage the child with spastic cerebral palsy to extend his legs and point his
toes down. They do not prevent him from crossing his legs, and unfortunately
the excitement of the bouncing movement causes the child to stiffen and adopt
the spastic position.

The child's bed should, if possible, be placed in such a way that attractive
features encourage him to turn his head away from his preferred side, so that his
position in bed does not favour any asymmetrical body postures. If there is only
one position in which the bed can be placed, changing the headboard to the other
end of the bed may be necessary. No eye-catching features, including the door,
should be on his favoured side otherwise he will keep his head turned to that side,
thus reinforcing deforming tendencies. It may be difficult or impossible for the
child to turn over in bed. However, he will become stiff and pressure points will
be uncomfortable if he lies in the same position all the time. It will therefore be
necessary for him to be turned over or moved several times during the night.
Loose, light garments and a lightweight duvet will make easier any movements
the child can make for himself, but care should be taken to ensure that he is
warm enough. The type of bed, as well as the bedding, needs to be looked at
carefully. For the child who throws his arms up and back at the shoulder or
thrusts his head back, a hammock-shape is essential. However, a real hammock
is a very unstable structure that the child will be unable to climb in and out of, so
a nest-shape may need to be made from an arrangement of firm bolsters and
pillows. Advice on sleeping posture should be sought from the physiotherapist,
with at least two alternatives to allow for changing the child's position during the
night. Details are not included here since the correct posture will vary from child
to child depending on the degree and effect of his condition.

Problems which may be encountered by this child in the activities of bathing
and using the lavatory are similar to those of other children with a physical handicap, and are discussed elsewhere in this book, but many children with cerebral
palsy have severe difficulty in accomplishing the extremely complex process of
feeding, which involves head, neck and trunk control, movements of the mouth,

tongue and jaws, and the swallowing mechanism. Self-feeding also requires precise and synchronised movements of the hand and arm, preferably bilaterally. Since these children are also likely to find speech difficult, it is the speech therapist who is the most skilled professional to seek advice from in all aspects of feeding. She will be able to demonstrate methods for overcoming tongue-thrust, dribbling, choking and other problems. For all these children, however, the basic rule is the same: careful positioning, method and atmosphere should make the best of the child's ability and co-operation and facilitate the feeding process. He should be leaning slightly forward with hips and knees well flexed, both hands in front of him and his head bent down a little. His trunk should be well supported, and strapping him into the seat by means of a pelvic band will ensure that hip extension does not propel him off the seat.

Seating is important at all times, of course, not just during meals. The Cheyne seat insert, made to fit onto a Major Buggy, will increase hip flexion and therefore decrease the likelihood of spasm. A useful hammock-shape can be achieved in a beanbag but this is not suitable for floppy children. Triangular or 'corner' seats will prevent shoulder extension, and straddle seats are useful against adductor spasm at the hips. Wedges and prone boards support the body while leaving the arms free for unrestricted movement.

Carrying a child with a stiff body or resistant limbs can be awkward and tiring. However, it can be made easier by handling him in the manner most likely to overcome his difficulties. Before he is lifted up, his body should be pulled forward so that he is well flexed at the hips. The child who stiffens into extension and crosses his legs will be helped to avoid this if his hips and knees are well bent and he straddles his mother's hip. The child whose arms and head fly up and back will benefit from being carried with his arms round his mother's neck and his head well forward over her shoulder. However, excessive carrying should be avoided, primarily because the child should be encouraged to use his own ability to move from place to place as much as possible and secondarily because his parents or carers must protect themselves from fatigue or injury, especially as the child grows heavier.

Learning to achieve independence in self-care is of great importance to the child with cerebral palsy, and his occupational therapist will wish to emphasise this. She will also be involved in developing his co-ordination, particularly his manual dexterity, and his powers of perception. To this end, she will advise parents on the choice and presentation of toys and play situations, and in preparing him for school activities.

A Child with a Limb Deficiency

Acquired and congenital amputation are the two terms used in the description of limb absence, a congenital amputation indicating that the child was born with part or all of the limb missing, and acquired amputation indicating that the loss of part or all of a limb was due to an accident or to surgical removal. The range of intelligence of children with a limb deficiency does not normally differ from that of the general population.

A child who has normal use of one upper limb may use an artificial limb to replace his other hand and arm. If both his upper limbs are deficient, he may become highly skilled at using his feet and toes for such activities as dressing himself, feeding and writing. He may learn to cook and take up hobbies such as art using his feet.

If part or all of his lower limbs are missing, his life-style will be affected in quite a different way. His ability to care for himself and to perform creative activities will not be impaired. However, his mobility will be affected to some degree. An amputation below one knee will have very little effect on his ability to move about, to indulge in such active sports as football, and to lead a normal life (apart from brief periods when he is getting used to a new prosthesis or if his stump has become sore or injured). If the amputation is above the knee, he should be able to walk well but his participation in sport may be restricted except for skiing and swimming. A child who has lost both legs below the knee may have similar restrictions on his sporting activities, and the child who has bilateral above-knee amputations may be considerably handicapped.

For all children with lower-limb deficiencies, swimming is an ideal form of exercise and an excellent way of using up energy, both essential to the less mobile child, but above all it is a sport in which the child can join his peers and compete with them. It should, therefore be encouraged in every way. Provided that attendance at the local swimming pool has been begun when the child is very young, there should be no problems of embarrassment at exposing the affected limb to the public gaze. However, all children are notoriously self-conscious at various stages of their lives, and parents must be aware of and sympathetic to their child's emotional difficulties. This child should also be encouraged to take up a wide range of less active hobbies which he can pursue into and through his adult life, should his mobility decline for any reason.

It is important for the child and his family to understand the need to incorporate any artificial limbs into the child's life as he grows and develops, so that he is enabled to acquire the skills relevant to his age at a normal time. Fitting of a lower limb prosthesis will prevent too much delay in early attempts at sitting, crawling, standing and walking. Once the child can sit, he should be wearing a simple upper limb to facilitate learning to crawl. By the age of six months a baby will use his hands freely and should have the use of an upper limb prosthesis for practising two-handed grip. A fixed hook terminal will be used by the child to pull himself into a sitting position and later to pull up to standing, and a split hook can be tried for the one-year-old. Children give all splints and appliances, but especially artificial limbs, very hard usage. Prostheses need to be strong but should also be very light, and they should be renewed at least once a year to accommodate growth and to compensate for wear.

The successful use of artificial limbs depends to a great extent on their being used from an early age, and this is only possible if the child's parents have accepted his disability and the need for him to use aids to lessen his future problems. The advantages to an adult, both socially and from an employment point of view, of having two functional upper limbs cannot be denied but can only be achieved by committed use from babyhood. The young child can only accept split hooks if his parents do. They must be made to realise that a hand is a tool, which enables a human being to touch, control and modify his own environment.

'Reach' is an association of parents and hand/arm deficient children which aims to improve the range, availability and supply of artificial limbs for children. It is involved in research and sends out newsletters to inform parents of new developments, and has set up mutual support groups throughout England and Wales. Details are obtainable from the secretary R. Hendry, 11 Shelley Road, St Marks, Cheltenham, Glos., GL51 7LE.

A Child with Muscular Dystrophy

There are several different kinds of muscular dystrophy, Duchenne being the most common. This form is a condition affecting boys which causes increasing weakness. It is important to avoid keeping the child in bed or immobile if he has Duchenne muscular dystrophy, as this may weaken him further. He should be encouraged to keep active, and his muscles and joints should be stretched regularly to keep them supple. The physiotherapist will show him the exercises he should do. He should be encouraged to sit upright with his feet flat on the floor and his legs parallel.

Gradually, the child will become more dependent on parental assistance in caring for himself. The strategy is for parents to keep him independent for as long as possible, but to recognise signs of frustration or fatigue and help him when he needs it. It is essential for him to be allowed to maintain his dignity and self-esteem even when he must rely on others to do things for him. He should be asked to choose what he wants to eat, wear or do, so that he continues to control as many elements of his life as possible. Above all, he needs to keep his role and status in the life of his family. His intelligence and his interests will not deteriorate, and he will continue to develop intellectually in the same way as other children of his age, even though his muscle strength is fading.

Lightweight bedding, simple clothing, and space in which to move about with walking aids or a wheelchair are all very important to this boy, as is time to perform those tasks which he can manage alone. The occupational therapist will advise parents as to what aids their son will require for the activities of daily living, and when he should have them. As he becomes more disabled, parents will need to take a closer look at their home and the facilities it offers, in the light of the suggestions made elsewhere in this book. Families should join the Muscular Dystrophy Group of Great Britain, Nattrass House, 35 Macaulay Road, Clapham, London, SW4 0QP, from which can be obtained a booklet *Living with Muscular Dystrophy*, written and illustrated by D. Collette Welch. It is excellent for giving information and guidance to the parents of boys with Duchenne muscular dystrophy.

A Child with Perthes Disease

Perthes disease is a destruction of the growth centre at the top of the femur, seen in children between the ages of four and eight years. Boys are more frequently affected than girls, and the primary cause is unknown. Treatment is based on protection of the hip joint whilst regeneration is taking place, by means of operation, immobilisation, or a combination of both. Although this condition is normally of temporary duration, the treatment lasting an average of two years, the wearing of plaster casts, splints or braces can be quite a handicap to a lively youngster.

Perhaps the most difficult form of immobilisation, from a practical management point of view, is that in which the child's legs are held in wide abduction. Although the majority of these children are able to walk, their walking distance will probably be limited, and it is difficult to devise a suitable seat for them. If the cast or splints permit full flexion at the hip they can sit on a normal chair provided each foot is supported at hip level. If hip flexion is not possible, then a straddle chair will need to be made in order for the child to sit upright. A bicycle saddle is the best shape for the seat, but the child's back must be supported and he must be strapped on as he is most unstable, not only sideways but from front to back. The seat should be mounted on four legs which are fastened to skis for optimum stability, and the child should never be left alone on this chair. If it cannot be used at the table for feeding and play, a tray can be made to fit on to it. It is a good idea to allow this child to lie prone on the floor from time to time, supported by cushions to prevent his cast from hurting him, to give him a change of position and an opportunity to play with wheeled toys.

If prolonged walking tires him, he may need a pushchair or a wheelchair. Unfortunately, many pushchairs have filled-in sides which make them too narrow to accommodate the extra width, or the seat slopes down at the back causing the child's feet to stick up in front, and canvas seats are unsuitable. This may necessitate use of a wheelchair, which can be obtained from the local Artificial Limb and Appliance Centre. The armrests can be detached if they obstruct the splints, but it is essential for the child to be strapped into the wheelchair. His feet must be supported to take the weight of his splints and to prevent their digging in to the backs of his legs. If he cannot flex to 90° at the hips he may need a pushchair in which he can lie almost flat such as the one made by Silver Cross, but a small child can be transported on top of several pillows in a large pram. Again, the child must wear adequate straps and should not be left unattended.

Once the period of immobilisation is over, the child with Perthes disease can look forward to a normal future.

A Child with Spina Bifida

The majority of children born with spina bifida have a lesion at the base of the spine, but some have a lesion in the neck region or elsewhere. It is usually those children with the former condition who are more severely handicapped. After the child has had an operation to close this, great care has to be taken to avoid infection of the wound before it has healed.

It is unlikely that a child with spina bifida will be able to control his bladder, because he can neither feel when it is full nor be able to tell when he is emptying it. There is a danger of infection of the system or of pressure on the kidneys in an incontinent child, and parents must be taught exactly how to care for their child's bladder and how to test his urine for signs of infection. As he grows older, the child may be offered an operation to by-pass the bladder so that his urine can be collected in a bag. This has the supreme advantage that he never has to have a wet bottom again and can say goodbye to nappies for ever. Parents are taught how to fit and empty the bag and care for the stoma. A specialised stoma nurse keeps in touch with the child as he grows up and gives advice. If such an operation is needed, it should not be put off since chronic kidney damage is avoidable by this method.

The child will probably have no control of his bowel either, but this is not such a serious problem. Many children open their bowels automatically about once a day. Mild constipation is not important but more moderate cases should be treated with a mild aperient or the use of a suppository. If the child is allowed to become severely constipated he may suffer from continuous leakage which is most unpleasant. He will then need an enema or manual evacuation and his bowels will become over-stretched. With proper management of such problems the child can be confident in normal society.

Weakness of the legs of a child with spina bifida varies in degree. Physiotherapy will be used to strengthen the muscles and to prevent the joints from becoming stiff. Sometimes operations will be carried out to enable good muscles to work more effectively, and once the healing process is complete the child must make full use of them. The physiotherapist will show parents the exercises their child must do and will teach him the correct walking pattern using any aids she may give him. She will also decide whether the child needs any type of wheelchair, and arrange for one to be ordered if required.

A child who has poor sensation in his skin is liable to develop pressure sores without feeling discomfort, and if he cuts or bangs himself he may not notice it. It is essential for the parents and child to know if he has this difficulty, and how to deal with it. Before he goes to bed each night, he should be taught to examine his legs and buttocks with the aid of a mirror. He must look for scratches, cuts, blisters, bruises or burns, and learn to keep his skin clean and dry. He must become wary of fires, radiators, hot water bottles and the corners of furniture, and must understand the importance of changing his position frequently to redistribute the pressure of his body weight. Insensitive feet and legs are inclined to be cold and should be kept warm by means of two pairs of socks and not by external heat.

The family should be encouraged to join the Association for Spina Bifida and

Hydrocephalus. Its aim is to give all possible support and help to those born with one or both of these disabilities and their families, through social work and welfare grants and by giving advice on the provision of aids and equipment, alterations to the house, education, independence and employment.

A Child with Hydrocephalus

Hydrocephalus is the term used to describe an excess of cerebro-spinal fluid within the ventricles of the brain. Under normal circumstances this fluid, which is formed constantly inside the ventricles, flows down the spinal canal and also between the ventricles and over the surface of the brain where it is absorbed. An obstruction in one or more of the narrow channels through which the fluid passes may cause a partial or complete blockage. It is estimated that the amount of fluid produced in the adult brain is about one litre every day, and unless this reaches the parts of the central nervous system at which it is absorbed there will be a rapid increase in its volume. This leads to an increase in the pressure of the fluid within the ventricles, which will result in abnormal enlargement of the head. It may occur either before or very shortly after birth, and the rate of growth will vary according to the severity of the blockage.

Provided that the condition is mild, or that treatment is given in the early stages, the child has a good chance of growing up normally. The rapid enlargement of the head will be arrested, and within a few years its size will be within average limits for the child's age-group.

The current method of treating this condition is to insert a shunt and valve to drain this excess fluid from the head into a blood vessel in the neck, and it is effective. However, the child with such a shunt needs extra attention to ensure that the mechanism does not become blocked or infected. Apart from inspecting the actual valve, it is important for parents to learn to observe clues in their child's behaviour which indicate increased pressure of fluid in the brain. Such signs as unusual drowsiness, vomiting, irritability, thirst or lethargy should lead to an immediate check on the condition of the shunt and valve.

A Child with Still's Disease

George Still gave his name to the condition of rheumatoid arthritis found in children under 16 years of age. Although the adult form affects about 5 per cent of the population, the juvenile form only occurs in 0.2 per cent of children. The joints of the neck, knees and wrists are most commonly affected in the child who is suffering from this condition, and a skin rash may appear and fade intermittently over the course of the illness. The joints become swollen but pain is not a major feature and therefore mobility can usually be maintained. However, it is very important for the child to get a good night's sleep, and to rest for about three hours each day. He should be encouraged to move around during waking periods, since contractures can occur in the affected joints very rapidly. Exercises will be taught as appropriate by the physiotherapist, and the frequency and duration of exercise periods must be adhered to most conscientiously since excessive exercise may cause undue wear and strain in the joints but too little may fail to prevent deformities from occurring. Hydrotherapy is a pleasant and effective form of exercise for all children with Still's disease.

A wide range of drugs is currently available to combat this condition, and new substances are constantly being sought.

In some cases the use of splints at night is prescribed, chiefly to rest the involved joints and to prevent contractures. Care should be taken in applying these, since tight fastening may cause circulatory problems but loose fastening will not allow the splint to fulfil its purpose. It is advisable for parents to check the splint before they go to bed to see that it is correct. A soft collar may be offered to support the head if the neck is involved. If a deformity cannot be avoided, then a series of correcting plasters may be applied to reduce the deformity.

Because the synovium in the joints of children is relatively thick, the end results of this disease may be quite reasonable and the child should be encouraged to lead as normal a life as possible.

CHAPTER 4

A Child With Special Needs

Educational Handicap

Educationally handicapped children are those whose intellectual development is very much slower than normal children. For this reason they are sometimes called 'the developmentally young'. In most cases they can only develop to a certain level though what that level is is difficult to predict. Many instances of educational handicap cannot be attributed to a specific or clearly defined cause, which makes the outcome impossible to forecast. On the other hand, some conditions of known origin affect different children in different ways, which again makes predictions difficult. Some forms of treatment may prove more effective in one case than in another, and new methods of care, treatment and training are being devised every day. This is why professionals are increasingly reluctant to state what a child's future condition will be. What they can do is give advice on how best to help him. The challenge for parents and teachers is to ensure that the child reaches his optimum level of development at each stage, so that he is in the best position for taking advantage of the future progress in treatment which is sure to come from the present research programmes.

More and more effort, time and money is being spent on the plight of the educationally handicapped. Better care for expectant mothers is already paying dividends, and new tests are constantly being developed to check the progress of the unborn child. The birth of a baby is the subject of a considerable amount of time in the teaching and training of doctors, nurses and midwives, thus reducing the likelihood of accidental brain damage occurring at the time. The newly-born are subjected to various tests to detect a wide range of known conditions, and their progress is constantly monitored. Much more is also known about the psychological needs of babies and those who care for them than was recognised only a few years ago, and more is being discovered all the time. With the wealth of information now available, fewer children are being born with handicapping conditions, and those who are unfortunate enough to do so are less likely to be affected severely.

The extent to which his condition affects his life varies considerably from one child to another. Some children will always be dependent on others to a substantial degree, unable to make decisions concerning their own way of life or unable to care for themselves. Some may eventually develop sufficiently to be able to live in the community with only minimal support. The majority will require a certain amount of care and supervision throughout their lives. It is up to those with whom the child lives, who determine his care and handling, his sociability and independence, and the acceptance and attitudes of family and friends, to ensure that he is given the opportunity to develop his potential.

The handicapped child has so much to learn. He must learn how to eat, drink, move about, communicate. He has to understand what is meant by good and bad, wet and dry, hard and soft, what is safe and what is dangerous, and he has to learn how to make friends. His primary training ground is his home where, as a member of the family, he must learn to behave in a socially acceptable way so that the family can retain its place in society. Useful social attainments like feeding and dressing are more important than academic achievement for such children.

It is useful to establish a routine as early as possible, and this has been described in Chapter 1. As the child grows older, his needs will change and the routine will need revising from time to time. However, routine should not be allowed to rule the household nor to degenerate into boring ritual. A certain flexibility should be built in so that the family can take advantage of special opportunities. If an invitation to coffee is issued at short notice or a long-lost

cousin arrives unexpectedly, they should not be ignored. There will be days, or even weeks, when the routine disappears completely for one reason or another. This may make for complications but should not last for long, and its lack should not be allowed to upset the family. Attempts at re-establishment can be made another day, but some missed opportunities may never offer themselves again.

Communication

Communication starts with the mother-child relationship and is normally an unconscious process, but in the case of the educationally handicapped child, the parents will need to give more deliberate encouragement, by keeping a note of what excites him, what appears to interest him, and what causes tears or temper. They should talk to him and sing to him, and make a fuss of him whenever he responds. They should speak his name when they go to him, and use simple, single cue words to accompany actions and activities, like 'up', 'wash', 'hands', 'toes', 'drink', and so on. The same words should be used for each action and the family as a whole should try to be consistent. Flooding the child with chatter will make it difficult for him to pick out key words.

As he grows and develops, language has to be made necessary in the child's dealings with his world. Before he can speak he should be encouraged to use sounds to attract attention and to indicate what he wants. Games that require him to make some sounds, such as rhymes and poems, will encourage him to listen as well as to speak. 'Pop goes the weasel' is an excellent example, as it cannot be completed until someone says 'Pop!'. With ingenuity, well-known rhymes and songs can be adapted and new ones invented, and a response should be demanded of him every time. The speech therapist is the primary source of advice in developing the child's communication skills, and if she does not think he will acquire adequate speech she may suggest teaching the family an appropriate sign language, such as Makaton.

The Child's Physical Condition

Unfortunately, many educationally handicapped children do not develop well physically. Sometimes this is due to the fact that their handicapping condition affects the body generally. But in a large proportion of cases there is no medical reason why they should not have normal physical development. In these children, their poor physique may be caused by fear of running, climbing, jumping and all the other body-building activities in which children normally indulge. The child needs to be encouraged to participate in these pursuits, so that he will learn to overcome his timidity and enjoy an active life to the full. He will become more healthy and robust if given the opportunity, and will also look better. When his contemporaries are starting to ride tricycles and go-carts, he should be given the chance also. However, all children are wary of strange things, and the handicapped child should be allowed plenty of time to study a new toy, walk round it, touch it and push it rather than be dumped in or on it and wheeled around.

Regular medical and dental checks are a necessary precaution. As well as their greater vulnerability, many of these children are less able to express those small signs which indicate that something is wrong. Routine visits of this kind also have the advantage of allowing the child to get to know his doctor and dentist, so that he will accept their intervention when it is necessary.

If a drug is prescribed for the child, it should always be given at the right times and in the right quantities. The effects of drugs depend entirely on the dosage and the frequency of administration. If parents are concerned about a drug's effects, they should write down their observations and report them to the doctor. It is dangerous to reduce or increase the dose, experimentally or by accident, and it is highly dangerous to double a dose when one has been missed.

In the same way, if the child has been put on a special diet it must be adhered to. If this creates problems, these should be discussed with the hospital dietitian, and if the parents find it expensive they can apply for financial help to meet the extra cost. Parents should be advised against trying out a variety of 'wonder-drugs' and 'miracle diets' without the whole-hearted approval of their child's doctor.

If the child looks well, with a clear skin, bright eyes and an alert manner, and his mother tries to give him a well-balanced diet, feeding should not be a problem. If he goes through a phase of eating very little but still looks well, the family doctor should check his condition. If the doctor shows little concern, then there is no need for parents to worry. However, this is a time when problems could begin. As with any child, if the mother starts pleading and trying various games to make him eat, she is really setting the wheels in motion for the child to learn the power game. If by refusing food he can make her more attentive than usual, even have her in tears or offering him bribes, then he will refuse food. A wise mother learns not to react in this way but to treat the situation with the utmost calm, offering small helpings of favourite foods and if they are rejected taking them right away out of sight. Food should not be offered too frequently, about once an hour is sufficient, and it should be left for a few minutes while mother is apparently busy with something else before being taken away again. In all probability this will soon prove effective.

Management of Problems

Fear

Many things that an adult takes for granted can be a cause of real fear to a child, and more especially to a handicapped child. While most parents will be aware that the first encounter with a train may frighten a young child, they will not always appreciate the potentially alarming experiences which are present in and around the home, magnified as they are by imperfect understanding.

Some children are frightened of the flushing cistern. The sudden noise and rush of water is alarming to them, and unless they are introduced to the sound from some distance away and reassured, this fear can deter them from using the lavatory. If a child has always used his potty in other rooms, his first attempts to use the toilet can be so threatening because of fear of the flush that it may become a considerable problem. In the same way the sudden blare of a radio, which should be switched on at low volume and slowly turned up, or a door bell or telephone bell, will startle a child, as will a dog's bark or a banged door. Very often, a child who cries out on hearing these sounds is told not to be silly, but he will only cease to react in this way when he has grown used to such noises and can understand their causes, and may always show his alarm more clearly than an adult does.

Fear of shadows, which may be unidentifiable or grotesque, is very common, as is fear of unusual movement such as billowing curtains. To a child these indicate the presence of a mysterious monster lurking in the room and preparing to attack, and great care must be taken to allay such fears. If the child is afraid of having his hair washed or going on a swing, he should be allowed to control the situation himself as far as possible. Perhaps he can try washing his own hair, with his mother standing by giving instruction and encouragement. At first the results will not be very good, but he will not come to any great harm if his hair is a bit messy for a few weeks and he will become more competent with practice. It will be preferable to going through a tearful ordeal for ever. For the swing, he should be allowed to explore it with no one near, and to get on in his own time. Often children begin by leaning over a swing on their stomachs, keeping their feet in contact with the ground. Later skills like sitting on the seat and kicking with the feet can be left until they have become more confident. Other such problems can be approached in a similar way.

Dogs are usually friendly and harmless, but their boisterous manner and exuberant greetings are terrifying to many young children. It is not enough to tell a child the dog will not harm him. He must be given time to watch it from a distance, preferably while being held securely, before being encouraged to make closer acquaintance. The time required for observation may vary from ten minutes to several weeks, and the child should not be hurried. Some children may never be able to relate to large animals. Small pets such as hamsters are usually acceptable, and perhaps part of the reason for this is that they are caged. A child should not be forced to handle them, since many people cannot tolerate the feel of fur or find small active creatures abhorrent.

There is another side of this coin. A child who is not exposed to new situations and experiences in case they frighten him is going to become over-timid and his knowledge of life will be restricted. Learning can only take place when given the opportunity, and some potential talents may never be discovered unless the child is encouraged to experiment. However, it is important that the child is taught to be on the look-out for danger. He must learn to beware of fire, cookers and other household hazards, and to take care when negotiating stairs and steps. If he is able to go out alone he must be taught how to cross roads, but if he cannot learn to cope with traffic he should never be allowed out unaccompanied.

Cot or Chair Rocking

This can be a real problem in several ways. It may damage carpets or walls, it may make a noise and upset neighbours or it may be very irritating for other members of the family. If the child cannot be prevented from doing it there are a few solutions worth trying. The first one is to fasten the cot or chair to the floor with strong screws. Another, more expensive, solution is to buy a rocking horse or a rocking chair which is mounted on a stable base, and fasten the base to the floor. This channels the rocking into a more acceptable form, as will a garden swing. If the rocking still persists at night and is disturbing everyone, it may be advisable to do away with cot, chair and bed and let the child sleep on a good mattress on the floor.

Head Banging

If the child bangs his head in his cot, bumper pads can be purchased which fasten to the cot rails, one for each end. If he does it in bed on the wall or headboard, a padded headboard can be used. In addition, a long piece of board can be padded and covered with a wipe-clean material and screwed to the wall alongside the bed. If he bangs his head on the floor, walls or furniture in any other rooms, there may be little alternative but to ask the hospital to supply a special helmet for him. Although it may look a bit strange, it can be disguised in a variety of ways with caps, bonnets and balaclavas. At the same time advice will be needed on how to prevent the child from banging his head. The simplest method is to distract him in some way when he starts, but this is much easier said than done and although it is essential to persevere in prevention attempts, the immediate concern must be to take precautions against the child's damaging himself.

Temper Tantrums

If the child exhibits a temper tantrum at home, the family should leave the room and close the door. If the room contains items of potential danger to the child, for example a fire, he should be moved to a safe room as swiftly and undramatically as possible, without speaking, and left with the door shut. If the child throws a tantrum in a shop or other crowded place, the principle of ignoring him is the same: the parent takes him outside or away from the crowd and then waits quietly until he subsides. If he lies on the pavement, he should be left there; his hands and face can be cleaned afterwards. A crowd is an interested audience, unfortunately, and their stares, gasps and offers of advice will only encourage the child to continue his display. If the parents can keep calm and wait until the tantrum is over, both they and their child will have taken a step towards preventing this behaviour.

   If the child holds his breath and turns blue, this can be very frightening. However, he cannot harm himself. Even if he holds it until he faints, the loss of consciousness will restore normal breathing anyway. If parents shout, slap, plead or cry they are rewarding this problem behaviour and it will increase in frequency and intensity; though it must always be remembered that these children, particularly if they are unable to communicate or express their needs, may suffer from intense frustration at times — and temper tantrums are not uncommon in normal children during the pre-school years.

General Discipline

If parents are to give their child continuous loving care, they have the right to expect his co-operation. If they know he is not trying, is not doing what he is capable of doing, then he must be shown that more is required of him. Parents should first ensure, however, that there is not some underlying cause for his behaviour such as fatigue or confusion or the presence of something which is strange to him. They should not allow their child to become spoilt out of pity for his handicap, because he will become more difficult for them and others to manage as he grows older and this may influence the way he is treated or the possibilities offered to him. The best way to cope with this is for them to try to anticipate problems and prevent their coming to pass, by distracting the child from a potentially difficult situation whenever possible, and to try to avoid unnecessary conflict. They should make sure that their requirements for good behaviour are reasonable ones, and that their child understands them. The youngster who is learning to walk will grasp anything which is handy when he wants to pull himself up. If he takes hold of his mother's skirt she helps and encourages him, but if he catches at the tablecloth she gets angry with him! The reason behind such seeming inconsistency is hard for a child to understand, and parents are well-advised to check their methods for similar inconsistencies if their child appears to be bewildered. Sometimes, however, there will be inconsistency for a different reason, perhaps because the patience which seemed so easy to display the previous day has been worn right down so that behaviour which was acceptable 24 hours ago cannot be tolerated today. In this case, parents should make allowances not only for their child's bewilderment but also for their own fallibility.

Conditions Requiring Special Care

Many of the conditions which may affect children have characteristics that indicate the need for special care. A brief outline of the 'special needs' of the more prevalent conditions are included below. In all cases, the child's doctor will indicate the care and treatment required by each individual child, and the advice contained here and in the rest of this book should be modified accordingly.

A Child with Down's Syndrome

Nearly a third of all educationally handicapped children have Down's syndrome. Although they all have a characteristic look about them, nevertheless they inherit some family features and no two Down's children are alike.

Down's babies are often 'good' babies, placid and lazy; therefore they need to be roused, stimulated and encouraged. They may not demand to be fed and they may not take much food unless pressed. They are also usually 'floppy' babies, whose muscles are too relaxed and whose joints are too mobile. Positioning of these babies is important, and the way they are carried will influence their physique. A kite-shaped nappy and side-lying will help to prevent laxity at the hips. The heart or lungs may be affected by the condition, and some have a reduced resistance to infection. Care should be taken to dress the child warmly, particularly his hands and feet, as his circulation may be poor. Another special need is to give great attention to washing his eyes; each eye should be washed separately with a clean swab or piece of cotton wool, and then dried separately with another piece. This should be done with one wipe only across the eye, from the nose to the outer edge.

It is vital that a Down's baby is stimulated right from the beginning, making him use all his senses. He will almost certainly become a happy, loving and affectionate child and a real member of the family. He can learn to feed and dress himself and can be toilet-trained. He can learn to speak and may be capable of learning to read and write, but it is important to give priority to teaching him the social skills of feeding, dressing and acceptable behaviour.

The Down's Children's Association was formed in 1970 and membership has many advantages. It is advisable for parents to join very early in the baby's life as its members offer one another considerable support and advice.

A Child with Epilepsy

Epilepsy occurs due to metabolic disorders or damaged brain tissue and there is a variety of causes. Some children are born with epilepsy but for some the condition may begin after a childhood illness. Despite popular prejudice, only a small minority of those with epilepsy are mentally retarded, and the effect which it has on the future of the child depends considerably on the severity of the condition and the way it responds to the drugs available. More than 80 per cent of people suffering from epilepsy live a normal, full and active life in all respects.

If a child suffers an epileptic attack of the *grand mal* type, he should not be restrained in any way. Collars, belts or other tight fastenings should be loosened as quickly as possible, and any furniture moved away so that he cannot injure himself. If this is not possible, the child should be moved quickly but gently to a safer place. His body will be stiff and tense to begin with, and then he will begin to shake or quiver. When these stages are over he will become limp and can then be picked up to lie on a bed or settee. He should be kept warm and comfortable and when he recovers consciousness it is important that someone he knows is near to reassure him as he may be confused or suffer from a slight loss of memory. These attacks are not seen often as few children have such a severe condition and modern drugs are effective in controlling the worst type of attack. The child is more likely to have a *petit mal* attack which involves loss of consciousness only. Care of the child after the attack should be the same as for *grand mal* however. Parents need considerable medical advice on matters relating to the treatment and care of their child, as epilepsy affects children to such varying degrees.

If an epileptic child is over-protected and not allowed to behave like other children in case he has a fit, he cannot develop normally. It may have such a depriving effect on him, in fact, that he will appear to be backward. Frequent absences from school may lead to difficulties in keeping up with his classmates. It may be necessary for parents to enlist the help of the child's teacher in giving him extra time in school or work to do at home, in order for him to catch up.

Families can join the British Epilepsy Association, Crowthorne House, New Wokingham Road, Wokingham, Berks., RG11 3AY, and obtain the Family Doctor booklet *Epilepsy and fits* which is published by the British Medical Association. The child should be encouraged to wear the badge of the British Epilepsy Association at all times, and to carry a card giving his home address, telephone number and details of any medicines he normally takes. If he is enrolled as a member of Medic-Alert, 9 Hanover Street, London, W1, he will be issued with a small metal bracelet to wear all the time, which will inform others of his condition in case of an emergency.

A Child with Diabetes

Diabetes is a condition in which the body is unable to regulate the amount of sugar in the bloodstream. The two main symptoms are the need to pass large quantities of urine and therefore the need to drink excessively. Treatment takes three forms: a carefully controlled diet, regular doses of insulin, and keeping fit. The child's diet sheet will be explained to parents by the hospital dietitian and should be followed meticulously. However, since diabetes is so well known and its problems are accepted universally, there is such a wide variety of specially prepared foods available in many shops that catering for a diabetic is not an onerous task. One of the most important points is that meals must be taken regularly, not at varying times, and that no meal should ever be missed.

As the child grows older, he must be taught the importance of taking regular meals and of avoiding certain foods. He can be shown how to test his urine and to administer his own injections, he should carry sugar wherever he goes, and be taught to recognise his own symptoms of low sugar levels and then to take sugar quickly. It is primarily the parents' responsibility to ensure that their child's teacher, and the parents of friends with whom he spends his time, know that he is diabetic and that they understand how essential it is for him to have meals at the correct time. They should also know what signs of low blood sugar to look for and how to cope with them.

The family should join the British Diabetic Association, 10 Queen Anne Street, London, W1M 0BD, and Medic Alert, 9 Hanover Street, London W1. The child will be issued with a small metal bracelet to be worn constantly, which will inform others of his condition in case of emergency. The Family Doctor booklet *Life with Diabetes*, published by the British Medical Association, contains valuable advice for diabetics and their families.

A Child with Asthma

Asthma is an allergic reaction to substances which are either inhaled or ingested. Some of the most common causative substances for the young child, are milk, eggs, nuts, chocolate, wheat and citrus fruits. The inhalants which cause the most trouble will cause asthma in a non-allergic individual, however.

Asthma can start at any age, in fact the age of onset often gives a clue as to the cause. Food allergies are indicated if the child is under one year old, household substances may be the cause in the child from one to five years and if the onset of asthma occurs in children over five, pollen allergies are the most likely cause. As children grow older they may develop greater tolerance to causative substances, but the opposite can also be true.

Emotional factors often play a role in precipitating asthma attacks in pre-disposed children, and if the emotion leads to crying or shouting this will produce spasm of the bronchial tubes which will worsen the attack. Attacks can occur under almost any circumstances, however, and can be very frightening. The child will sit with his shoulders hunched, looking very anxious and struggling to breathe. His lips and fingertips may turn blue, and his whole body will be tense.

The course of asthma varies from one child to another and cannot be predicted, but treatment can alleviate the condition to a considerable extent. The first steps are to make the child's bedroom as free from potential causes as possible by replacing feather and flock pillows and quilts with those made from synthetic materials. Blankets, rugs and carpets made of felt, wool and other animal hair must be removed, as must elaborate curtains which may harbour dust. It is also advisable to use similar measures in the rest of the home, and to avoid furred or feathered pets or to house them out of doors. Skin tests may be useful in indicating some of the substances which are affecting the child, and attempts at reducing his sensitivity to these can then be made. Children are taught correct breathing methods and exercises, and the physiotherapist will also demonstrate postural drainage to the parents. Respiratory infections should be treated as early as possible. During an asthmatic attack, medication is usually given orally to relax the lung tissue and sedatives may also be offered.

Calm and reassuring handling of the child, particularly during an attack, is important and care should be taken to avoid any fuss or drama concerning his condition.

A Child with Cystic Fibrosis

Cystic fibrosis is a condition in which the mucus is abnormally thick. A diagnostic characteristic is the high level of salt in the sweat of affected children, which can cause problems in the summer. The lungs, which normally have a thin layer of mucus, become clogged so that there may be difficulty in breathing and infections are slow to clear up. In severe cases this can lead to destruction of the lung tissue. Excess mucus is also found in the digestive system, where it may block the intestine. The pancreas does not secrete enzymes and therefore some foods, especially protein and fat, are not adequately absorbed.

Early diagnosis is essential, and treatment must be carried out diligently in order for this child to thrive. A high input of physiotherapy, meticulously supplemented by the parents, helps to alleviate the respiratory condition. This therapy will include breathing exercises, coughing, postural drainage and percussion of the chest, and must form part of the child's daily regime. Treatment of the digestive disorder involves regular intake of pancreatic extract and a special diet. Even when pancreatic extract is taken orally, food absorption is still somewhat inefficient so that a high protein diet coupled with supplementary vitamins is indicated. Salt intake should be increased, especially for very active children and also during periods of hot weather.

Provided the lungs remain undamaged, this child can be cared for quite adequately at home, and can expect normal growth, social life and schooling. The Cystic Fibrosis Research Trust was founded in 1964 and plays a central role in helping and advising the parents of children suffering from this condition.

A Boy with Haemophilia

Haemophilia is a hereditary condition in which blood clots very slowly. One of the major problems is bleeding within the larger joints, which are subjected to considerable stress in normal life. Another is that of prolonged bleeding from minor cuts, and internal bleeding from knocks which have not broken the skin. The heart and lungs are well protected by the ribs, but the abdominal organs can be damaged rather easily. Any signs of bruising of the head, neck or abdomen must be reported to the doctor immediately, as must traces of blood in the urine.

Furniture corners should be padded or rounded off while the baby with haemophilia is learning to crawl and walk, and every effort should be made to ensure that the furniture he holds or sits on will not tip. Padded cot-sides and padded bars round his pushchair, will help to protect him and the doctor may advise the wearing of a crash helmet to prevent bruising his head. As the child grows older, he can be taught to be aware of his needs and encouraged to protect himself from knocks as far as is practical. He should be prevented from participating in games where he may be knocked by other children or by bats and balls. However, he should be encouraged to develop physically and socially as far as his condition will allow, and should participate in swimming (not diving) and a wide range of less active hobbies.

A Child Who is Over-active

The most difficult time to care for an over-active child is at night. All the other members of the family are ready for their sleep but the child is still wide awake. He probably seems to need far less sleep than anyone else and his parents may wonder how he manages to keep active for 20 hours a day or more. Whilst the difficulty of the problem is not underestimated, there are a few suggestions which may help them to cope.

A regular bedtime routine is indispensable for an over-active child. The time at which he is put to bed is not as important as the method, though it is usually easier if his parents don't try to put him in his bedroom until late in the evening. Time and patience are required in preparing the child for bed, and the right atmosphere has to be created deliberately. It helps to have soothing music playing (of the slow orchestral type, not fast or stimulating), with the volume restricted to soft background music. His mother or father should undress him in dim light in a warm room, washing him gently. They can talk in a low voice, and perhaps sing or read a short familiar story. Once he has been put to bed the child has to learn that, should he get out again, he will always be put back. It is best to observe the same routine every night, even to the same story or piece of music if the child requests it, as anything new will only serve to over-stimulate him.

The child's bedroom needs to be a particularly restful environment. It could be decorated in blues and greens, for example, with soft carpet and thick curtains, avoiding if possible, pictures, mirrors, ornaments or pattern in the room. Furniture should be fixed in position and there should be no open shelves. Windows should be barred and fastened securely, and their opening should be restricted. If this limits ventilation, a grille can be let into the door or into the wall over the door, allowing ventilation from the landing. If parents are afraid that the child may roam in the night when they are asleep, a bolt can be fixed on the outside of his door, but the door should then have a panel of reinforced glass inserted so that the child can see out and his parents can peep at him from time to time. The bolt should only be secured just before the last person goes to sleep and undone as soon as someone wakes up. The room itself must be cleared of potential dangers and the child left with plenty of soft toys, comics and magazines to amuse himself with. However, he should never be locked in his room as a punishment or he may refuse to go to bed at all. It may be that the doctor will prescribe sleeping pills for the child, in which case their effects should be carefully monitored. If he considers that other members of the family require more rest, he may prescribe some for them.

The over-active child needs a variety of activities to occupy him and space to release all his energy. A strong swing and climbing frame will help, and if he can be taken swimming or horse-riding he will probably enjoy these. If he feels tense he may start hitting out at other people or the furniture. It is possible to purchase a 'punch clown' or similar toy which will right itself when knocked over and provides an acceptable target for aggression. An alternative is to suspend a punch bag from a tree. If he likes to bounce or jump on the furniture, such activity should be confined to an old mattress in the garden or perhaps to a small trampoline — but only under supervision.

Some of the advice given above may sound a little extreme, but the excessively active child can present problems that come near to destroying the family which is struggling to retain him in its midst.

CHAPTER 5

Independence For a Handicapped Child

The more independent the child can become, the more he can participate in the normal way of life. Independence will give him self-respect and dignity and the opportunity to develop the attitudes and interests which contribute to his own personality. Increasing ability to care for himself will gradually relieve the burden on those who have been caring for him and improve his chances of becoming totally independent. At school all children are taught such skills as reading, writing and counting. It is a waste of teaching time for them to have also to be taught how to wash, use the toilet, and dress, and so these things should be learnt at home. The amount of skill a child acquires in the activities of daily living will depend to a considerable extent on the amount of encouragement he is given at home.

Learning is a slow process which includes elements of trial and error, patient guidance, repetition, experience and practice. Throughout his attempts to do things for himself, the handicapped child will need a loving attitude, calm support and attention. These will give him the security and the confidence from which he can develop his need for independence. There will be times when he will feel very frustrated, as all children do, at being unable to accomplish something for himself: these are the times when he needs extra love and understanding.

For some handicapped children the use of a special aid may help them to perform a certain task, but aids need to be used with discrimination. To deny a handicapped child the use of any aids may mean that he has to struggle in pain or remain dependent on another person for help, but to allow him to use an inappropriate aid is at best a waste of money and at worst may cause or aggravate deformities. The best person to seek advice from is the occupational therapist who will assess the child's needs and abilities and then give guidance on the aids that may be appropriate. Since the child's need for aids will change as he grows and develops, the therapist will reassess his requirements at regular intervals and review the aids he is using.

Feeding Himself

Learning to eat and drink without help, and practising the art until one is able to do it without making a mess, requires considerable co-ordination and skill. In order to make it as easy as possible, the child should have suitable equipment scaled down to his size. Adults can prove the importance of this point for themselves, by trying to eat a meal using a carving knife and fork, a serving spoon and soup ladle, and drinking from a two-pint jug! Inevitably there will be problems in controlling the large knife, they may hurt their mouths with the large fork, or dribble when using the big spoons. Similarly, it will be found almost impossible to drink from a wide-necked heavy jug without allowing the liquid to run down the chin. It is a useful habit to analyse personally what the child is being asked to do, to ensure he is going about it in the easiest possible way.

As soon as he can put his fingers in his mouth, the child is ready to begin to try finger-feeding. If he is still quite young he should be given soft cheese or biscuits which will crumble without choking him. However, if he is already able to bite and chew he can be given apple or carrot pieces.

The child must be sitting as upright as possible, in a chair which fits him well and holds him straight and with a harness which prevents him from falling out. He should have a large tray or table which comes up close to him and is on a level with his waist. It is not a good idea to give him a stiff plastic bib as these affect movement and are often most uncomfortable. A deep plate with steep sides is easier to take food from than a shallow one with sloping sides, so most cereal bowls are suitable. It is possible to obtain a plate surround which will clip on to a shallow plate to give it extra depth, but a deep dish looks more normal. To keep the plate from sliding, a piece of dycem or damp plastic foam can be used underneath it, or one can buy a bowl that has a suction pad on its base. The latter is particularly useful if the child tends to pick up his plate and throw it down. If he takes a long time to feed himself, it is worth buying a plate which has a hot water compartment. His meal can then be kept warm and appetising so that perseverance is rewarded; it would be a shame for him to struggle to feed himself and be rewarded by cold, congealed food.

Back row, left to right: Tommee Tippee scooper hot-plate, Mothercare stay-warm plate, Tommee Tippee double hot-plate
Middle row, left to right: Mothercare non-slip cereal bowl, Tommee Tippee scooper-plate, Tommee Tippee scooper-bowl, Boots cereal bowl
Front row, left to right: Boots non-spill bowl, Manoy small Melaware plate on Dycem grippistrip, Boots trainer plate

If he cannot grip an ordinary spoon, the child may be able to put his hand inside a looped handle. Alternatively, a piece of tubing pushed over the spoon handle to enlarge it may make it big enough for him to hold. If it is not clear which hand he prefers or which one gives him more control, a spoon can be tried experimentally in either hand until the signs of preference emerge. Long handles, or handles bent round at an angle to the bowl of the spoon may assist a child with limited movements to get his food from plate to mouth. A pusher may be useful in loading his spoon, although pushers seem to have gone out of fashion. The bowl of the spoon should be small, as it is very difficult not to be a messy eater when using a large spoon. The child should progress to a fork as soon as possible, but not a metal one as the prongs may hurt his mouth until he is able to control his movements. A plastic fork, either a baby one or a small picnic fork, is more suitable at first. To make feeding easier for the child, food should be made

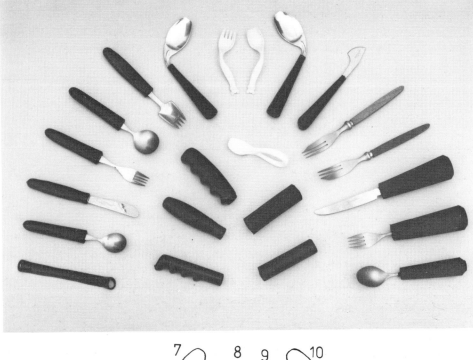

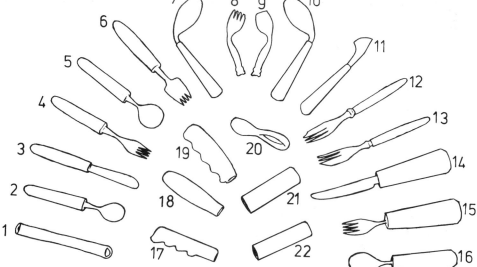

1. Sunflower Selectagrip handstrap
2. Sunflower Selectagrip baby spoon
3. Sunflower Selectagrip knife
4. Sunflower Selectagrip fork
5. Sunflower Selectagrip round spoon
6. Sunflower Selectagrip Splayd
7. Manoy left-handed spoon
8. Tommee Tippee fork
9. Tommee Tippee spoon
10. Manoy right-handed spoon
11. Manoy rocker knife
12. Left-handed Dinafork
13. Right-handed Dinafork
14. Ultralite knife with large handle
15. Ultralite fork with large handle
16. Ultralite spoon with small handle
17. 18. 19. Sunflower Selectagrip handles
20. Tommee Tippee baby spoon
21. Large-bore Rubazote
22. Small-bore Rubazote

thicker than usual. Cereal or custard can be mixed fairly stiff, and juice drained from stewed fruits. Food that will adhere to the spoon gives the child the best chance of getting it as far as his mouth.

Back row, left to right: Walt Disney two-finger-handle hat mug, Manoy Melaware beaker, Evoware Selectacup with adjustable handles
Middle row, left to right: Tommee Tippee spouted mug, Boots mug with trainer lid, Tommee Tippee weighted cup, Walt Disney straw-cup
Front row, left to right: Flexistraw, Boots baby training beaker, Embee invalid feeding cup, Plastic tube through pencil clip

A two-handled mug is the easiest to hold, provided the handles are big enough to put his fingers in. For independent drinking, a mug with a spout is preferable when he is trying to hold the mug himself, even if he can drink from a normal cup held by someone else. By using a spouted cup, neither parent nor child will be so afraid of spills, and if the child tips the mug too much the spout will control the flow and prevent him from choking. If he cannot lift a drink at all, a pencil pocket-clip can be attached to a cup and a piece of transparent plastic tubing inserted into the spring. Provided the cup is fixed securely so that it will not tip, he can then suck the drink through the tube. Between meals the tube should be submerged in a sterilising fluid such as Milton.

Any child learning to feed himself will make a mess. If a plastic sheet is placed on the floor under his chair, and he and his mother protect their clothes with large aprons, they can concentrate on independent feeding without fussing. However, although adequate preparation and use of the right equipment are elements in successful self-feeding, the major requirements are patience and perseverance on the part of the adult. The reward is the child's greater social acceptability.

There are many ways in which a child can practise the skills needed for feeding himself while he is playing. Digging in the garden or in a sand pit, mixing and stirring, help him to develop the manipulation of the hand-held tool. Water play also teaches him to lift, tip and pour, as well as showing him how liquids behave, and all children love to hold tea-parties for their toys, pretending to feed them with spoon and cup. There are endless possibilities for play in all these activities.

Dressing Himself

Because undressing is much easier than dressing, and parents usually have more time to spend with the child before he goes to bed than first thing in the morning, independence in undressing and the comparatively simple task of putting on night clothes makes a logical beginning. It takes a normal child several years before he is able to dress himself without assistance; for the handicapped child it is likely to be an even more protracted process.

The safest place for the child to be whilst coping with the intricacies of manipulation and balance is on the floor — preferably a warm corner with a soft carpet, and without much furniture so that he cannot bump himself if he rolls over. The technique is to begin by pulling garments almost off him and then encouraging him to give the last tug. He should be praised when the garment is

off so that he is rewarded for his effort. Gradually the adult should do less and less of the work until the child has taken over, ensuring that it is always the child who gives the final pull and achieves the success. If his hands are not very strong, it may be that he can do more by using teeth, feet or chin, but the adult should ensure that the child does not experience too much frustration. Once he is progressing well with undressing himself, he can be expected to start dressing. At first he will only be able to co-operate by keeping still or holding out his arms and legs, but gradually he will begin to pull garments on. Again the adult will do most of the work but allow the child to finish the task, so that he gets plenty of pleasure out of helping. If there is a problem which is causing him great difficulty, there may be an alternative. One type of fastening can be substituted for another or perhaps eliminated altogether, or clothes of a different style may be adopted.

Dressing himself can be a tiring activity for some time as it involves considerable manipulation to get clothes on at all and great concentration to get them the right way up and the right way round. For the child to maintain persistence, he needs plenty of time, gentle encouragement and liberal praise when the task is accomplished. It is important not to overtax the child, and he should never be asked to put something on and take it off more than once each day. Repeated practice in one session is both boring and unnecessary since he will be practising every day for the rest of his life.

It will help the child to put things on in the right order if they are laid out for him one on top of the other with his underclothes coming to hand first. It is not easy to assess which way round garments should go, and the label commonly found at the back of the neck is not usually a sufficient clue for the young child. A coloured tag on each sleeve may answer this problem, but if this method is used, the same colour code should be used on every garment. He can be encouraged to be tidy, to fold his clothes and put them away, if adequate storage space is provided within his reach, and lots of praise is given for trying to do what is being asked of him.

Dressing-up has been enjoyed by generations of children, and provides practice in learning all the small skills that go to make up this everyday task. Plenty of brightly coloured clothes and a big mirror are required, and it is advisable to shorten adult garments to prevent the child from tripping over them. Add hats, bags and shoes if the child can walk normally. Strings of beads or other items of jewellery are better excluded for safety's sake. Dressing toys is also a favourite pastime, but should not be attempted with small toys as it can become frustrating. Dolls' clothes are often expensive to buy but can be made very simply out of scraps of material.

Choosing Clothes

It is most fortunate to live in an age which has drip-dry, easy-care, machine-washable and stretchy fabrics available for clothing. Gone are the days of bleaching, starching, crimping and fluting. Children now wear clothes designed for their way of life, whereas up until the turn of this century they were dressed in unsuitable, heavy garments based on adult styles, and toddlers — girls and boys alike — had to learn to walk under several layers of petticoats. The last decade in particular has seen a revolution in dress for adults as well, such that nowadays the casual, comfortable and practical styles are more popular than the formal. This means that girls no longer have to wear frilly frocks to be accepted in society but can conceal their calipers with smart trousers, and that small boys can cover their splints with long trousers at an early age instead of having to wear shorts in order to conform. Capes and ponchos are acceptable, and are much easier garments to put on than coats, and shoes are now available in such a variety of styles that special shoes are less noticeable. All these developments can be exploited to help the handicapped child towards independence in dressing.

One of the chief considerations is to try to eliminate all fastenings from the child's wardrobe, since they are fiddling and time-consuming, and to aim instead for elasticated garments which pull on. Those garments which must have fastenings should always do up in the front. Zips are fairly easy to fasten, especially if they have a large ring on the grip, but open-ended zips are very difficult to locate. Toggles are usually easier to hold than buttons. Buttonholes can be sewn up and replaced by elastic loops, and buttons are easier to manipulate if they have a long shank. Cuffs can be fastened together permanently by a piece of elastic. Velcro is a useful substitute for some fastenings but it is not easy to close it flat. Instead of using a length of it, small squares can be attached at intervals along an opening; the sides can then be matched without creasing. If each pair of squares is made from a different colour of Velcro, the child will be less likely to fasten the wrong pieces together. Neck openings need to be generous, and armholes should be deep with raglan or Magyar sleeves. Shoes should be slip-ons rather than buckled or lace-up, if possible.

The most suitable clothing materials are those which are soft and stretchy, warm and comfortable. An active child keeps warm but a child whose movements are restricted becomes cold very easily. Thermal underwear, though expensive, is excellent. Care has to be taken to avoid belts, pleats or seams which come under the child's thighs or buttocks when he is sitting down or which he will be leaning on. Back fastenings can also cause discomfort.

If the child is in a wheelchair, it is necessary to guard against any of his clothing being caught in the wheels. Tassels and fringes should be avoided, and in the case of girls, skirts should not be too full. Flared trousers may need elastic in the hem or bicycle clips to keep them away from castor wheels. The child with crutches or calipers also needs to avoid clothing which may become caught up.

Protective Clothing

Cuffs are often subjected to considerable wear and tear by the child who uses crutches or a wheelchair. Office clerks used to wear sleeve protectors to keep ink from their clothes, and it is easy to make some from a tough cotton or plastic material. They are just simple tubes, gathered in by elastic at each end. Leather cuff-binding can be stitched on to coats and jackets, but has to be removed for washing or dry-cleaning. Leather patches are useful not only for elbows but also for knees, and can be sewn inside trousers where calipers rub. However, these too must be removed for washing so washable iron-on patches may be preferred.

In cold weather, it is not a good idea to wrap a child in blankets since his mobility will be restricted. He will remain warm but keep more mobile in extra layers of clothing. A combination of thermal underwear, trousers, jumper and track suit will insulate him effectively, and will allow for greater activity. If he is confined to a wheelchair, he will keep warmer in a leg-muff than in blankets. There are now larger sizes on the market, similar to the push-chair muffs which have been available for some years, which keep out draughts.

There is a wide variety of rainwear in the shops and parents should not experience great difficulty in obtaining something suitable for their child. If the children's wear shops do not seem to have the right answer, a camping shop or a cycle store will have a range of cagoules, cycling capes and other similar articles which may suit the handicapped child's special needs.

Underclothes

Vests with an envelope neck mean that the child will not experience difficulty in getting them over his head, and those with large armholes are recommended. Pants and knickers need to be slightly baggy rather than tight fitting, with elastic at the waist but not necessarily in the legs. If the child wears calipers or splints or is in some kind of plaster, it may be necessary to open the side seams of pants and sew tapes or Velcro on each side in two or three places. They can then be removed easily for changing or toileting. A pliable fabric such as stretch towelling is ideal for underclothes. Petticoats or underslips are not essential everyday wear, and are only another item for the child to contend with.

Indoor Clothing

Shirts, blouses and cardigans should be avoided, since their fastenings are far too costly in terms of time and difficulty. Preferable are jumpers, pullovers and ponchos, with no buttons, poppers or hooks. Polo necks need folding down neatly so they too should be avoided. Crew, turtle or vee necks are a more sensible choice and should be combined with raglan sleeves. There are two ways of putting on a vest or jumper, by pulling it over the head first or by putting the arms in first. The latter method is the one most children find the easier, since they are more likely to put the garment on the right way round and less likely to put the head through an armhole. Lay the garment face down on the table in front of the child with the waist nearest to him. He should slide each arm into the adjacent sleeve, and put it over his head by raising his arms. This will be easier if he can get the sleeves well up on his arms before trying to put his head into the neck opening. If the child has very short arms, cap or cape sleeves make an attractive alternative to sleeveless garments.

Ties are unnecessary: they are a problem to do up, clip-on ones are difficult to attach, and ties on elastic can be dangerous.

Skirts, shorts and trousers are simple to put on if they have elasticated waists. A skirt can be put on over the head if this is the easier method for a girl, and for a boy wearing calipers it is possible to open the gusset and inside leg seams of his trousers completely and close them with zips, tapes or Velcro. Another way of accommodating calipers is to open the side seams of trousers and fasten these with open-ended zips. Pulling trousers up over calipers is very difficult as they catch on the buckles, and it is not very good for the fabric. For the child who has difficulty in bending, long tapes can be sewn to the waist of knickers, skirts and trousers with which to pull them up; the tapes can then be tucked into a pocket. A wraparound skirt is easy to put on, but fastening it may be a little difficult. Track suits are always useful.

If the child's waist is not very clearly defined, or if he wears a body brace or corset, it may be difficult to keep lower garments from slipping down. Stretchy, colourful braces permanently attached to the waistband, which can be slipped on the shoulders, may solve this problem. A one-piece dress is often easier for a girl to put on than a jumper and skirt, and if it has no waistline it will disguise an awkward shape such as a surgical support, stoma bag or deformity. Most suitable is an A-line design which flares from the shoulders, or a smock. For the bigger girl, many maternity styles are ideal in this respect.

Outdoor Clothing

It is a good idea for parents to purchase outer garments a size larger than the child normally wears, to give more room when putting them on. Capes and ponchos are exceptionally easy and may even be made up Redskin-style to be suitable for a boy to wear. A short coat will be more comfortable for the child in a wheelchair than a full length one, as there will be fewer folds of material to sit on. As already mentioned, large toggle fastenings are preferable to buttons and a ring-pull will make a zip easier to grasp. Many coats have hoods attached and these should have elastic rather than drawstrings round them, so that they can be pulled on without needing to be tied.

Gloves can either be sewn to the end of sleeves with elastic or, for ease of washing, can be sewn to each end of a long elastic which is then tied on to the coat's hanging loop so that the gloves dangle through the sleeves. Tape should not be used for this as there is not enough flexibility. Mittens are easier to put on than gloves, but once on they are a hindrance to dexterity. If the child needs to handle money or anything small when his hands are covered, he should wear gloves rather than mittens. If he propels his own wheelchair, a leather patch can be sewn to each glove where it gets most wear, in order to make it last a little longer.

Footwear

It is possible to buy socks which have a different colour in the toe-cap and heel-turn from the rest of the sock. This may help a child to recognise and locate them

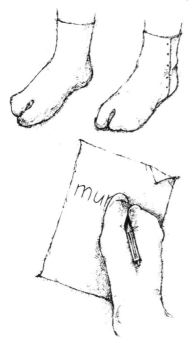

the right way round and therefore without rucks. A child should never be allowed to put shoes on over wrinkled socks, especially if he has paralysis or poor circulation of the feet, as they will rapidly cause sores. For girls, tights are best avoided as they are just another layer to remove when visiting the toilet. Knee socks and a soft, thick skirt or trousers are just as warm. Japanese socks called *tabi* are divided in such a way that the big toe is separated from the other toes (see illustration). These are a boon to the child who has to use his feet for manipulation as he can hold pencils, brushes, cutlery and other small items between his toes.

Properly fitting shoes are desirable for all children but essential for the handicapped. Clarks and Start-rite provide the greatest range of sizes and promote care in fitting. The child's feet should be measured at least every six months and larger shoes purchased as often as necessary. This is not an area in which economies should be made, but parents who need financial help may receive this with the aid of a social worker. If there is a marked discrepancy between the sizes of the child's feet, Clarks operate an odd-shoe service. Surgical shoes are often a great problem. If the child needs to have shoes made especially for him it can take up to six months for them to arrive, by which time his feet may have grown: this is one time when parental pressure is needed to improve the service.

If the child is not walking at all then he can wear slippers at the discretion of the physiotherapist. They should be boot-shaped, that is they should cover the child's ankle bones, and fleecy so that they warm the whole foot as much as possible. The inactive child suffers considerably from problems of cold and poor circulation in the feet. Slippers should not be too small as cramped toes also become very cold.

It will probably be easier for the child to put shoes and socks on with his foot up on a stool than with it on the floor. This will be particularly useful if he has a stoma, if bending forward makes him feel giddy or lose his balance, or if he is overweight. If he has difficulty in deciding which foot is which, the shoes can be placed side by side on a cork tile or piece of card and drawn round. Then, if the tile is set in front of the child and he is shown how to match the shoe with its outline, each shoe will be in front of the appropriate foot.

It is easy to forget how important appearance is to a child. If he has to wear special shoes there are ways of making them look more attractive with a bit of imagination. For the young child, attaching toy eyes, ears and nose to each shoe may do the trick, or adding a bunch of bells. The slightly older child may fancy pom-pom balls, a smartly fringed tongue or a big, bright square buckle over the top. Surgical shoes can be coated with a brighter colouring without too much difficulty. Scuffing is a big problem, especially with a child who walks unevenly. 'Scuff-kote' is an excellent preparation for hiding the scratches, and if the shoe becomes badly marked it can be given a new lease of life by covering it with shoe dye.

Learning to tie laces is an unnecessary activity for a child who can wear normal shoes since there are plenty of slip-on or buckle-and-strap designs available. Unfortunately, laces are often used for surgical boots, calipers and artifical limbs so children using these will have to master the art sooner or later. It is an aid to learning if two short laces of different colours are stitched together for each shoe. They should be threaded the same way in each one so that, for example, the white lace comes to the right hand and the black lace to the left hand in both shoes. Instead of practising while bent double with the shoe on his foot, the child can start learning with the shoe on a table — facing the same way as his foot, not pointing towards him. There is a simple method of tying laces with one hand, and elastic laces are available which do not have to be undone. Unfortunately, elastic laces are only suitable for shoes and not for calipers.

Caring for Himself

Almost everyone enjoys a warm, leisurely bath. Water is soothing and supporting to the body, and warmth is welcomed by tired, stiff muscles. For children, the bath has the added attraction of affording a great opportunity for play, hence the variety of bath toys that can be found in any toy shop. As long as he is not getting cold, the child should always be allowed to play in the water for a few minutes so that he looks forward to his bath.

Most bathroom taps are stiff and many have several facets on them which makes them difficult to grip. If they are too awkward for the child to manage, the occupational therapist will supply a lever adaptation so that the child can turn them on himself. Getting into and getting out of the bath are the most difficult and dangerous activities a child has to master when learning to care for himself. There should be an adequate non-slip mat beside the bath as well as one in it, and the child should be taught to sit on the rim of the bath and swing his legs in rather than to step over the side. If he cannot balance on the rim, he could try sitting on a board which fits across the end of the bath. Once sitting with both feet in the water, he can lower himself in, or on to a half-way bath seat and then into the water. Board and seat can both be removed while he washes himself and then replaced for him to reverse the procedure to get out safely. If the child is unable to get in and out by this method, he may need a Mecanaids Autolift in order to be independent of help. There are several seats which are suitable for use as support within the bath (see p. 8) and these can be supplied at the discretion of the occupational therapist.

Once he is in the bath the child should be encouraged to go through all the motions of washing himself. If he can use only one hand, it is possible to make him a mitten with a soap pocket or to cut a slit in a fat sponge and put a piece of soap in that. If he has difficulty in reaching between his toes or behind his back, a long flannel with a loop each end, a long-handled brush or a sponge dish-mop may help. While he is trying to wash himself, his attendant can check that awkward and important areas are not overlooked. The child will probably enjoy rinsing himself with a hand-held shower nozzle or with a rubber shampoo spray pushed on to the bath taps.

The child needs to be sitting on a firm chair or on the floor when drying himself. The latter is safer since he can roll to get at parts of his body instead of trying to balance, but the floor must be warm and free from draughts. He needs a large, soft and fluffy towel to wrap himself in, plus a small one to dry the extremities. His clean clothes should be close at hand.

The hazards of bathing, especially for the handicapped child, are such that no child should be left to bath alone unless it is absolutely certain that he can come to no harm.

If a child suddenly takes a dislike to the bath, screaming and yelling on being taken to it or even at the mention of the word, it is probably wise to dispense with the traditional bath and settle for an all-over wash. In many older homes people have no alternative but to do this. Parents should be prepared to wait several days or even weeks before trying a proper bath again: if the child still rejects it they can set about reintroducing it by various means. If the weather is warm, an inflatable paddling pool in the garden with about three inches of water and a few toys in it will reintroduce the basic idea. The child should not be undressed as he will quickly realise what is going on, but be wearing the most easily washable clothes he possesses. He can be allowed to play outside without his attention being deliberately drawn to the pool. Within a few hours, or possibly a few days, he will be splashing, paddling or even sitting in it. Another way of getting him back to the bath could be to organise a few water-play parties. The mothers of two or three other children can be told the reason for the party and asked to participate. All the children need to be suitably clad. Warm water is run into the bath and plenty of toys added, including plastic cooking utensils. Only the visiting children are invited into the bathroom to play: the reluctant bather should not be taken in but left to join the others in his own good time. It is important for an adult to be in the room throughout to watch for accidents. Of course, providing he is washed thoroughly a child could go without a bath for years. However, 'de-sensitising' him, which could take anything from a few days to several weeks, is worth the trouble in the long run. Bathing is much quicker than a strip wash so the child is not going to feel cold so quickly, a warm bath is more soothing and therefore better preparation for bed, and the attendant will expend less time and energy if the child is in the water.

If he cannot reach the wash-basin, a sturdy and stable platform to stand on or an adequate chair on which to sit will be needed. There should also be a mirror close to the wash-basin, hung low enough for him to see himself with ease, and his own flannel, toothbrush, comb and hairbrush. If these are all the same colour they will be easier for him to identify. A nailbrush fastened inside the wash-basin by suction cups will be a boon to the child with only one hand or limited use of the hands, and soap on a rope or magnet will keep it from slipping or being dropped. Toothbrushes, combs and hairbrushes can all be fastened to pieces of dowelling or wooden coat hangers to make them longer, or can be pushed into rubber tubing to make the handle fatter. An electric toothbrush is a possibility for the child who cannot make the brushing movement.

If he can manage it himself, the child should be allowed to wash his own hair. He will probably require help for some time, as it is such an awkward procedure, and may find it easier to do in the bath. Alternatively, the kitchen sink is more spacious than a wash-basin and the adjacent draining board will hold the things he needs. Hair fashions, particularly as regards length, fluctuate very much, but short hair is far easier for a child to manage. It is advisable to have short hair cut well so that it looks attractive.

Using the Toilet

As the words 'toilet' or 'lavatory' are currently recognised, accepted and shown on most signs, private euphemisms can be a great embarrassment for a child who may have to communicate his needs to others frequently. If he cannot say the conventional word, he can be taught to make a specific gesture, and the parent should use the word and gesture together every time the child visits the toilet. The most obvious gesture is for him to place his hand over the lower abdomen, but this is not always acceptable socially. One alternative might be to raise the hand, as this is often recognised as a request to leave the room for toilet purposes.

A lavatory can be a frightening place for a young child. The lavatory pan is large, the cistern makes a loud noise, and water suddenly splashes and gurgles. Also the room may be remote from the living room and the family. It is important to ensure that it is not bare and gloomy but as attractive as possible. Many children have to climb on to a chair by putting up one knee and then the other and turning in order to sit. This is impossible to do on a lavatory, so there should be a small sturdy platform for the child to step on to so that he can sit on the lavatory without help. This should not be in front of the lavatory but round to one side — preferably between the lavatory and the wall. The child can then sit sideways on the seat, holding the cistern handle for support if it is conveniently situated or holding a short grab rail fixed to the wall. By giving him support for his feet and something to hold on to, the fear of falling in — which hinders many children's attempts at independence — will be eliminated. A trainer seat, made by Mothercare or Cindico, will make the hole in the seat smaller and therefore give more support to the buttocks, and if the child needs extra security a Mecanaids Toilet Aid which fastens to the lavatory pan can be installed. Although it has to remain in place once fixed, the arms fold away so that it does not impede use of the toilet by the rest of the family (see illustration).

If the child cannot wipe himself adequately and is unlikely to be able to do so for some years, it may be worth considering the purchase of a special bidet unit which attaches to the lavatory pan, in order to give him independence in toilet care. Everyone is entitled to privacy in the lavatory, and a child will lose a great deal of personal dignity every time someone else has to wipe his bottom.

Independence About the House

There are many ways in which the child's home can be modified to help him to be independent in it, without impairing it from the point of view of the rest of his family. In fact the majority of the concessions that have to be made to his handicap, for example siting switches at waist height or installing a lavatory downstairs, may make life easier for them as well. Once again, however, it will be parental patience and encouragement which will be the key factors in determining the child's ability to cope with his environment. Unless he is ill or over-tired, once he can make his own way from room to room he should be left to do so and not carried. Once he can climb the stairs unaided he must, although an adult should hover close behind until he is proficient. It is only by mastering mobility in his own home that he will be able to face visiting someone else's house with confidence, and only by experiencing a variety of home environments that he will be able to face the challenges of school and community without fear.

CHAPTER 6

A Handicapped Child in the Family

Each member of a family has his own problems, and the presence in the family of a handicapped child may add to these. The father worries about the family's financial situation, about keeping his job, about lack of sleep, and about the strain on his wife. The mother is concerned about her husband's disturbed nights, her ability to care for their handicapped child, and the needs of their other children. Grandparents worry about the extra work the parents must manage, and about the burden which their own increasing frailty may add. The handicapped child is struggling to cope with his special problems, and his brothers and sisters are picking up the stresses and tensions around them. The important thing for each one of them to recognise is that all families, whether or not they have a handicapped member, have to come to terms with similar feelings.

Because of the extra care he needs, the handicapped child can be instrumental in splitting the family into two segments, one consisting of the mother and the handicapped child and one consisting of the father and the other children. This upsets the balance of family life. It is essential, both for him and for his family, that the handicapped child should not be allowed to become the most important person in the household. Although it is possible for his parents to view the situation in a mature way, and to make allowances for one another's difficulties, the other children may be having a hard time of it. The chief problem is that while giving extra attention to their special child the parents may be overlooking the needs of their other children, perhaps expecting them to achieve independence at an early age, to take a large share of the household chores, and to help to care for their brother or sister. The handicapped child may be praised lavishly for something which is a major accomplishment for him, whilst the achievements of the other children may be overlooked because they do not seem so significant.

The Role of Father

The role of the father-figure differs to some extent from one family to another, but there are some areas of family life which most fathers recognise as their own. The first one is the role of partner, companion and protector to his wife. In modern society this partnership is one of sharing, of give-and-take, and of mutual support. It is clear from recent research on depression in women that those with young children are an especially vulnerable group. The birth of a handicapped child increases that vulnerability. The mother needs emotional support in order to face the fears and worries of caring for a handicapped baby, and practical help in order to meet the extra physical demands which are being made on her. It is rare nowadays for fathers not to assist with household chores and shopping, or expect to take their turn in caring for the children. With a handicapped child this kind of practical help becomes a necessity: but more is required than that. It is easy for a mother to become permanently housebound, with her mind perpetually focused on the child. It is up to her husband to ensure that she goes out, keeps in touch with her friends, and reinforces her independent personality by maintaining her interests.

On the other hand, there is a need for realistic adaptation, particularly in standards of household management. There is still a tacit mutual expectation that the wife who is at home all day will keep the house in good order. An important form of support from the husband is his explicit recognition that this may not be possible, and his appreciation of what is achieved. Mental stress is not due, in the main, to profound psychological problems, but to a sense of failure to meet implied demands such as these.

A husband's support is especially important when his wife has to face special ordeals, such as taking their child to the hospital for tests. If he can get time off work to go with her, not only will they both be able to hear what the doctors say and discuss it with them, but he will also be able to help his wife to manage the journey each way. If there are any decisions to be made, they can be made jointly rather than the mother's shouldering this responsibility alone. It is important for both parents, and for their child, that they face the future together on an equal footing. This will help to reduce the effect which the extra stress will put on their relationship.

One of the worries that has to be shared is that of finance. If the wife has been working until shortly before the birth of the handicapped child, the loss of her income will require careful budgeting. As well as the Family Allowance, there is special financial assistance for families with handicapped children, and this can take a variety of forms. The local authority social worker can help parents to sort out the legislation and ensure that they receive the benefits to which they are entitled. She can also ensure that parents apply for them at the correct time, since some allowances only become payable when the child has reached a certain age. There is still a considerable reluctance on the part of parents to seek out, let alone claim, their entitlements; therefore professionals have an important role in intimating to them that they, their relatives and friends have been paying contributions all their working lives to ensure that such State Benefits are available.

The role of father is, of course, very important to his child as well as to his wife. Whatever one's views on role differentiation, there are some activities which can only be met by a father-figure. Fathers and their young sons and daughters all over the world enjoy a special kind of play, often referred to as 'daddy-play', which is happy and boisterous. It usually involves daddy in lying

on the floor and being crawled over, and on the child being swung, carried on the shoulders and turned upside down! Unless the handicapped child is very fragile or sickly, he should experience this kind of romping frequently as it helps him to learn control of his neck and body muscles, to learn about coordination, and to gain confidence.

Once the child has become confident in playing with his father in this way, he can then be introduced to other activities that require plenty of movement such as the swing, climbing frame and pedal car or cycle. Father and child will both enjoy ball games and other outdoor pursuits like gardening, and with his father to encourage him, the child will become more adventurous. All these activities will develop the child's strength, surefootedness and balance. If the child is educationally handicapped, such encouragement may mean that he will be able to obtain pleasure all his life from sports in some form or other, being able to take part in jumping, racing or ball games. If he is physically handicapped, it is no less important to develop what strengths he has, and to introduce him to alternative pleasures such as the study of nature, train-spotting, bird-watching or photography. Swimming is great fun and excellent exercise for any handicapped child.

The father of a handicapped child is probably better able to decide what aids the child needs to make his life easier or more fun than any other person. One father, who has now become famous for his inventions, has made special wheelchairs for his limbless son, and another has designed and produced cycles for the handicapped since his child was born with spina bifida. Whatever a father's skill may be, he can get a great deal of fulfilment in helping his child to overcome his handicaps and to get the most out of life.

Occasionally, the father of a handicapped child considers that he has a pressing need to take time off work — if his wife is taken ill, his special child has to attend a significant appointment, or one of their other children has a special need. It is important that the professionals who are involved with the family should understand the worry this may cause. In spite of the wish to support his wife and family by his presence, the father may be anxious not to jeopardise his job. Although many employers are most understanding when they know the circumstances, many fathers do not feel free to ask for time off — something that professionals can usually take for granted.

Brothers and Sisters, Relatives and Friends

The rights of the special child, to love and affection, shelter, food, warmth, security and opportunity have been considered elsewhere in this book. But his brothers and sisters, relatives and friends also have rights, and the family will suffer if these are not met. The main ones at risk are the other children in the family, and their needs cannot be overemphasised. Parents should try to give them a pattern for living which closely resembles that of other families with whom they come into contact. They need to be allowed to develop their own personalities, and require the same opportunities for playing and learning as other children do. It is all too easy to subjugate their needs to those of the handicapped child. All children have times when they need extra loving, such as when they are tired or unwell or undergoing the additional stress caused by a change of teacher, an exam, or some other factor. They also have the right to come first on special occasions. It is important that they are given undivided attention on Open Days or Speech Days, birthdays, and when they take part in a school play or concert. If the only way parents can manage this is to hand over the care of the handicapped child to someone else for a few hours so that his brother or sister can have priority, then this should be done.

Similarly, the family's relatives and friends also have the right to come first occasionally, on birthdays and anniversaries, when facing a personal crisis, or if they are ill. They will not expect parents to abandon their normal responsibilities but will appreciate support and assistance, however limited, at their time of need.

Advice for Mothers

The mother of a handicapped child, or the person who fulfils her role, is the individual who is most likely to be giving him day-to-day care, all day and every day. Because of the demands it makes on her both mentally and physically, she is in danger of neglecting herself. But by doing this she undermines her own resources, a matter which her family, friends and those professional workers involved with her child need to be conscious of.

Her first priority must be physical fitness. Adequate food and rest are essential for housekeepers, cooks, home helps, chambermaids, teachers and nurses, and the mother of a handicapped child is all of these. She needs to pay attention to her own health and mental attitude and consciously set herself a list of 'rules', for example:

(1) Eat sensibly. It is important to eat balanced meals at regular intervals. This may require a little effort but is essential to physical well-being.
(2) Take proper rest and relaxation. This may mean going to bed at the same time as the children do, especially if the parents are likely to be disturbed during the night. Opportunities for short naps can often be used to advantage.
(3) Reduce or eliminate smoking and drinking. Their effect on physical and mental alertness and efficiency is considerable, and may be detrimental to the child's care.
(4) Keep morale high, by maintaining personal appearance, taking an interest in the world outside the home, and setting realistic objectives for the day with regard to housekeeping standards.

To these could be added: avoiding strain or injury to the back. Not only in caring for her child, but also in performing household chores, the mother's back is very vulnerable. Wearing sensible shoes, rather than high heels or slippers, will protect her posture and therefore her back and also avoid the danger of falls. When bathing the child or attending to him in bed, it is advisable to adopt a kneeling posture. Most mothers do too much carrying and often try to carry their child far more than is necessary. If the child can move at all he should be encouraged to take himself from room to room; if not, then he or indeed any heavy load should be moved on wheels — pram, push-chair or sturdy trolley — whenever possible.

Reducing the Chores

There are a variety of ways in which some of the time and energy spent on household chores can be reduced, thus releasing the extra time and energy that will need to be spent on the child. Some new methods can help, some old methods can be improved on, and some chores can be eliminated altogether. Not all of these involve spending extra money, but observing such household tips as the following:

(1) A simple time-saver is to pour a capful of liquid detergent into the water every time the bath is used. This will save cleaning the bath as it prevents scum and 'high-tide' marks from forming.

(2) Another chore to miss is cleaning the oven. By using a covered roasting pan or covering an open one with foil, splashes can be avoided. Non-stick saucepans also save scouring time, and a good soak should remove any food that does happen to get stuck.

(3) Scrubbing and polishing floors take a great deal of energy. It is worth giving them one good clean and then coating them with a polyurethane seal, so that in the future they will only need wiping with a damp cloth. This also applies to polished furniture which can be sealed in the same way.

(4) Perhaps the most time-consuming chore for the modern housewife is ironing. Many items of clothing and household linen can be bought 'drip-dry' and 'non-iron' and should be treated as such. If 'drip-dry' articles are pegged out carefully and hung up to air and store they will not need any ironing, and there is no need to iron underclothes or nightwear. Time spent on ironing towels or tea-towels is wasted since no one but the family will see them. Nylon fitted sheets not only need no ironing but also make bed-making easier. Use of tablecloths can be eliminated altogether, and the entire family can use tissues instead of handkerchiefs.

It is possible to reduce the time and energy (and fuel-consumption) required in cooking with a little forethought. When roasting a meal, sufficient can be cooked for the next day and any spare space in the oven used to make cakes or scones. A few more minutes spent on this session may mean that the main meal next day can be produced in as little as ten minutes. Another cookery time-saver is the use of convenience foods. They *are* convenient, albeit a little expensive, but if they help a family to enjoy a good nourishing meal without using precious time that could have been better employed, it is worth spending the extra money from time to time. If the family has a freezer, it makes sense to cook as much as possible in one session and freeze the surplus for days when there is a visit to the hospital or to a relative, or when some other activity reduces the time or energy available. The advantages of owning a freezer, in terms of bulk-buying and cooking ahead, are considerable to the mother with little opportunity to make frequent shopping trips and little time to spend on meal preparation. The average family needs at least ten cubic feet of freezer space and larger sizes cost very little extra. It should be kept in or near the kitchen if at all possible since access to it will be required several times a day.

Other major items of time-saving equipment are an automatic washing machine and a tumble-drier. If the child's difficulties mean extra washing it is better to go without a lot of other things in order to acquire these. A dishwasher is a great boon, but is still considered to be an expensive luxury in most households. It is often possible for families with a handicapped child to receive special grants for such major pieces of equipment, for example from the Rowntree Trust. A 'luxury' item may be a necessity for families coping with special needs.

Shopping can be a considerable problem if the mother is more or less housebound, but alternative arrangements can usually be made since many home delivery services are available. The local grocer may be willing to make a weekly delivery of all regular needs, such as tea, butter, sugar, cereals, washing powder, toilet rolls and so on, and the milkman often carries a range of other foods in addition to milk and cream. Full use should be made of any door-to-door tradesmen such as the baker, greengrocer and fishmonger. A telephone is a great help towards avoiding shopping trips, and use of mail-order catalogues can be an easy way to purchase clothing and household items. Occasional shopping trips should be organised carefully for maximum achievement. It is worth planning the route from shop to shop to take the shortest time, and trying to get as much as possible from a single shop. If the trip is to be concerned chiefly with buying clothes for the handicapped child, his measurements should be checked beforehand so as to reduce the time and energy spent in trying on.

Stress

All individuals and all families experience stress due to a variety of causes, one of which may be the difficulties of child-rearing. The extra problems involved in bringing up a handicapped child can be especially stressful, and an awareness of the need for constructive management is necessary if the family is to avoid breakdown. No one can take more than a certain amount of stress, therefore it is wise to try to reduce as many additional stress factors as possible. Such major upheavals as moving house or such problems as unemployment or bereavement, are acknowledged causes of stress, but some factors which will cause extra stress in any family are not generally recognised. These include:

Major shopping expeditions	Too many visitors
Changes in routine	Redecorating
Financial problems	Hospital appointments
Illness in the family	Difficult neighbours
Disturbed nights	Planning a holiday

All these and many very minor matters nevertheless add up, especially for the mother. Signs of stress are sleeplessness, headaches, irritability, tension and indigestion. If the mother is suffering, then the other members of the family will also be suffering, and action must be taken.

The management of stress is largely in the hands of the family itself, and that includes making adequate use of outside aid, from friends and relatives as well as from professionals. Asking for, and accepting, help is something everyone finds difficult but many people enjoy giving assistance and gain considerable satisfaction from doing so. Someone living locally who is willing and able to look after the child at short notice should a crisis occur, is invaluable. The mother who has an accident in the home or experiences some other sudden emergency, perhaps involving one of her other children, is in urgent need of this. But regular and routine help is also of great importance. Parents are wise to train a number of relatives, friends and neighbours to assist in the care of their child in the roles of baby-sitter, playmate, walker or teacher. It would be a mistake to overuse one or two willing helpers who, in any case, may not always be available when needed. It is the parents' responsibility to teach these people their own normal methods so that the child's care is consistent, and to make them understand that confusion is not good for him. The relief of stress which comes from knowing that help is there if needed raises the morale of parents considerably and fortifies their capacity for coping. The community is one of the family's greatest assets.

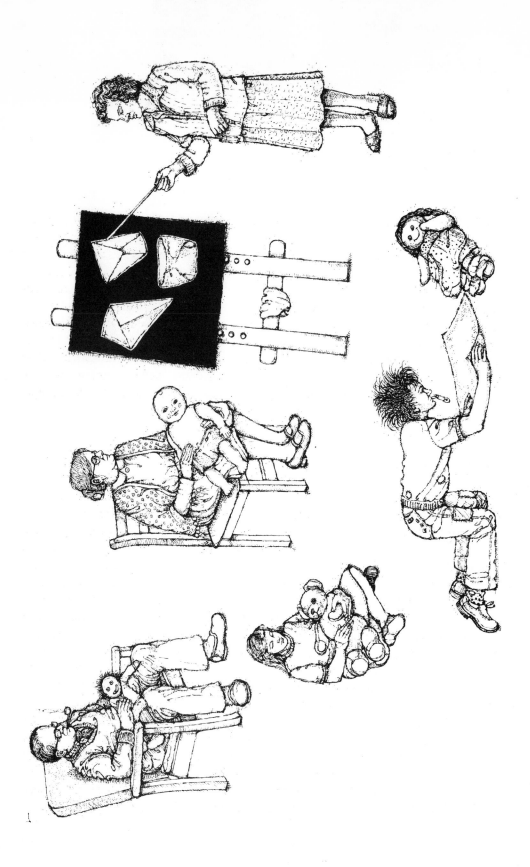

CHAPTER 7

A Handicapped Child in the Community

The child and his family are members of the community in which they live and their lives will always be bound up with the lives of the people around them. It is up to the adult members of the family to make and maintain relationships with the other people in the community on behalf of their children and for the sake of their children's future. But the community is composed not only of people but also of facilities. Judging by the present trends, it would appear that the children of today have to look forward to more leisure time than their parents or grandparents ever considered possible, and new communities are beginning to make preparations for this by developing the appropriate facilities. Therefore it will be necessary for parents to ensure that their child is able to take advantage of these preparations when the time comes, by seeing that he is an accepted and acceptable member of the community.

Social Acceptance

From the moment the baby is born, relatives and friends will be gathering round. They will be enquiring after mother and child, sending or delivering messages and gifts, and wanting to know the baby's name. As soon as possible they must be told about the baby's handicap since delay will only magnify the difficulties. They will be upset and anxious to help, but above all they will not want to upset the parents further. They will not know how to behave and will look for clues from the parents themselves. If the parents encourage their visits and show that they want people to see and get to know their baby, they will understand this as a wish for acceptance and for everything to continue as normally as possible, and will act accordingly. If they are pushed away at this stage, it will be difficult to make contact with them again later on. The situation should be explained to them and they should be helped to understand that the child will need extra loving care from everyone he meets. Parents also need to show that, because of the child's special problems, they and the rest of the family will appreciate the extra support they are offering, both now and in the future.

The next step is for the parents to take the baby out and, when they meet neighbours and friends, to tell them in a straightforward way about the baby so that future meetings will be open and unembarrassed. This is easy to say and not at all easy to do, but it is essential if the parents are to avoid becoming housebound by apprehension. Even so, they may have to get used to stares or tactless remarks when they visit new places, especially as the child grows older, but local acceptance and understanding can counterbalance this. It is useless to blame people for their prejudice. Parents need to help the people they meet to understand and sympathise with the problems which face families such as theirs. The only alternative is to keep their child indoors for ever, denying him — and the rest of the family — the right to a full and normal life.

Visitors to the home are an important part of a handicapped child's social experience, but people may stay away because they feel that parents have enough on their hands. Unfortunately, this only increases the family's isolation, so visitors need to be encouraged. All visitors will want to get to know the handicapped child but may need some gentle guidance on how best to approach him. Almost all children are wary of strangers and may dislike being petted or handled. A disabled child may be particularly anxious if he is held by someone with whom he is not familiar. Parents may need to exercise tact by explaining, for example, that the child has a poor sense of balance, or cannot feel that he is being held, or that he has been handled by too many strangers in hospital.

Potential visitors will appreciate being guided as to the best times for visits and the need for some advance notice. Most people want to do the right thing and will understand the need for extra consideration.

Another important contribution to social acceptance is in the field of behaviour. Behaviour which is even mildly unacceptable in the child will not only endanger the social life of the family, but will also mean that those who participate in caring for the child will derive less enjoyment from their tasks, and perhaps give up sooner. Every effort should be made to prevent such behaviour, either by determining what causes it and eliminating the cause or by distracting the child as soon as it begins. If this proves to be very difficult, or the behaviour is particularly bizarre, the advice of the doctor should be sought. There are a number of different strategies which can be employed in overcoming many problems and even the smallest improvements will be well worth the effort. To allow poor behaviour to continue, when the child is capable of better, bodes ill for the future of the entire family. Every child has to live in the society in which he is born, and if he is to lead a happy life in that society he must be acceptable to its members.

Outings

If the family has had to develop rather a complicated routine in order to care for the child and to manage the household chores, any changes in that routine will need careful planning. This does not mean that changes should be avoided since families have to learn to be adaptable and tolerant against the day when a change is essential. In fact, a common problem among handicapped children is the monotony of a dull and unrelieved routine. He should be taken out as much as possible so that he can experience all the things that a normal child experiences.

Family outings are especially desirable in that the members will benefit from each other's company and the stimulus of new surroundings. If a visit is planned to the library, the swimming pool, the cinema or a large department store, it is a good idea for parents to telephone beforehand and ask what is the best time to visit without being caught in crowds, which entrance to use, whether there is a lift suitable for a pram or wheelchair, and the location of the nearest car park. This approach often produces a very kind and helpful response, smoothing out many potential obstacles. However, all outings should be viewed realistically to ensure that they will be worthwhile. A balance has to be struck between giving the special child a wide range of experiences and exposure to the outside world, and accepting some limitations in terms of effort and stamina. For example, if the seaside is a two-hour drive away, the cost of such a trip might be better spent on an inflatable paddling pool which can be used in the garden on innumerable occasions. It should also be borne in mind that children's tastes are not very sophisticated, and that an afternoon spent on the platform of the local railway station will open up a new world of sights and sounds and a whole range of additional vocabulary to a child, as opposed to a drive along a concrete motorway cooped up in the back of a car.

The Practical Aspects of Going Out

The child whose handicap does not prevent him from walking without tiring is at a great advantage, and so are his parents. But most handicapped children need

wheeled transport for some part of their lives, or at least on some occasions. Because there is such a variety of prams, push-chairs and wheelchairs, selection is very difficult. Parents first have to consider the type and frequency of their outings. If they have a park and shops nearby and like to go out often, the child can enjoy the luxury of a large pram or well-padded wheelchair. If the shops are some distance away but the family has a roomy car, the choice could be a sturdy push-chair or a folding wheelchair. But if it is necessary to negotiate one or two buses, or even a train, and this has to be done quite frequently, then the child will have to sacrifice a certain amount of comfort in order to make the journeys easier to manage, otherwise his parents will not be able to take him out at all. The best choice in this case would be a Baby Buggy or a Major Buggy (see illustration). These can both be supplied by the Department of Health and Social Security, as can all wheelchairs, and the occupational therapist will advise on the most suitable one and arrange for it to be ordered.

If parents are selecting a pram or pushchair themselves, they should look for the following points:

(1) Can the child lie back and sleep in it, and sit in a good position?
(2) Is it long enough to last as the child grows?
(3) Will it tip easily if the child wriggles?
(4) Will it protect the child in bad weather?
(5) Is it wide enough to accommodate a coat and blankets when the weather is cold?
(6) Is there adequate fastening for a harness?
(7) Is the handle a comfortable height for pushing?
(8) Is it possible to see over the hood when it is up?
(9) Are the brakes adequate?

It is also important when pushing a heavy child that two of the wheels should be of the castor type. To push a loaded pram, or a child in a wheelchair, without having to tilt or jerk it constantly, there should be only two fixed wheels, with the others capable of turning in all directions. Regrettably, there are still many wheelchairs and a high proportion of prams and pushchairs with four fixed

wheels. They are very difficult to push and tiring to manoeuvre, and the tilting required in order to turn them makes for a very uncomfortable ride.

If a child's transporter also needs to carry a lot of shopping it should not be located in such a way that the vehicle becomes unstable. If the shopping can be packed round the child without making him uncomfortable, and he cannot harm himself if he interferes with it, there is no problem as this part was designed to take a load. However, dangling shopping baskets on the handle will upset the balance dangerously. A tray underneath may take some of the load, but otherwise shopping will have to be carried. Since it is awkward to push the pram with only one hand, it is easier to carry the luggage across one shoulder, or distributed over both shoulders in a rucksack. Of course, this is not only an excellent way of carrying heavy hurdens such as shopping, but also of carrying a small child. Women in some countries have used similar methods for centuries. Provided that any sling, back-pack or front carrier gives the child adequate support and protection, and provided that the mother can take the weight when it is distributed in this way, there can be no easier method of taking a small child with her wherever she goes.

If a heavy child has to be carried from room to room and lifted into a car or wheelchair, it is probably worth buying a trans-sit-seat, which is similar to a Moses basket but a larger fabric version. Designed to take a person weighing up to 13 stone, with strong carrying handles incorporated into the construction, it has a good harness and bar handhold for the passenger. It will prove invaluable when the child becomes too heavy for one person to lift alone (see illustration).

For some children, however, the problems of going out do not derive from lack of mobility but from too much. The active child often tends to run ahead, to bump into obstacles or to dart into the road without any consciousness of danger. It is essential that he wears reins in the street; in fact it is a great pity that the wearing of reins by all small children seems to have gone out of fashion. Of course, they do not solve all the problems and the child still has to be taught to hold his mother's hand and to beware of traffic, but the road is a dangerous place and until he has acquired adequate control he must be protected from being in, or causing, an accident. The streets are not the place for children to find out dangers for themselves or to 'learn the hard way'.

Outings by Car

When a child is taken out in the car, his safety must be the first concern. Obviously he should never be allowed to travel sitting on someone's lap on the front passenger seat, as this is the most dangerous place in the car. While he is small enough to lie in a carry-cot, he should be fastened into it by means of a harness and the carry-cot must be fastened to the car — Mothercare sells a carry-cot restraint harness. As soon as he is sitting up he should have his own car seat. There are many on the market and the following safety features should be observed:

(1) All fittings which fasten it to the car must be strong and properly installed.
(2) The seat must give the child firm, close support up to the top of his head.
(3) The harness must fit the child without allowing him to slide under it or his shoulders to slip out.
(4) The harness must be of wide or padded webbing, with no sharp edges.
(5) The release buckle must come undone instantly and be clearly labelled so that a stranger can release it, but it must be child-proof.

On even the shortest journey that child should be fastened properly into his car seat and the straps and fixings checked. When he has outgrown the car seat, his future needs will have to be considered. If he is too handicapped physically to sit unsupported in the car, it is possible to buy a car seat specially designed for the older disabled child. It is made by Britax and is known as the Handicapped Child Seat. If he does not need such support, a suitable child's safety belt can be installed. Kangol's child safety belt is the only design available at present which meets the following criteria:

(1) Pelvic padding.
(2) Prevents shoulders from slipping through due to A-shape of harness.

Britax Handicapped Child Car Seat

Kangol Child's Safety Belt

(3) Quick release buckle.
(4) Adequate fixing provision.
(5) No sharp edges to parts.
(6) Estate car conversion (optional).

The best time for a child to travel by car is at night when he is likely to sleep through most of the journey. Provided this arrangement suits the rest of the family, it is worth trying. However, whatever time of day it is, the child will probably sleep through part of the journey. The chances of this happening can be improved if the child is made really comfortable before setting out, that is dressed in soft, warm clothes with no uncomfortable buckles, pleats or creases, surrounded with pillows, cushions or folded coats, and covered with a soft rug. If he is leaning against part of his safety harness a little padding will prevent chafing. When he is awake it may be possible to keep him amused by offering a little toy from time to time, and picture postcards are also useful since they take up so little packing space. The journey should be planned to allow for making several stops at safe places on the way when everybody, including the special child, gets out of the car to stretch their legs and breathe a change of air. If the child is liable to be travel-sick, the GP should be consulted for advice on what he can be given: Kwells or Joy-rides are suitable for most children.

If the child is severely disabled, parents can apply to the local Social Services Department for an Orange Badge which will entitle them to certain car parking concessions. They can also join the Disabled Drivers' Club on their child's behalf, and will then receive a lot of helpful information concerning local amenities.

The handicapped child cannot always participate in a family activity. To expect him to do so may be asking too much of him, and to deny that activity to the rest of the family because he cannot share in it may be asking too much of them. Sometimes he will have to remain at home. As long as he is being cared for competently by someone he knows, and everything he needs has been left ready, the parents can go out and devote their time and energy to the rest of the family with a clear conscience.

Holidays

Holidays are very important — the freedom from chores, the break with routine and the change of environment will seem to recharge batteries and help families to keep fit enough to continue to care for each other. There are facilities to enable people to enjoy a holiday with their handicapped child, ranging from adapted caravans at the seaside to special hotels and hostels. Most organisations for the handicapped run schemes of their own, and social workers or occupational therapists should be able to tell parents about others. However, if a child needs maximum attention it may be so difficult to care for him in strange surroundings that the stress incurred will outweigh the benefits of the holiday. If this is the case, it may be better to consider making arrangements for the child to go to a residential centre while the rest of the family go away. Parents are often reluctant to take this step, but if the mother struggles to carry on without a rest until her health breaks down altogether, then the child may have to go into permanent residential care. Because this need is now more widely recognised, there are a number of residential centres that offer holidays and short-term care to handicapped children. They will also offer such help when a crisis occurs in the family, for example if a grandparent is taken ill or dies and the mother has to be away for a few days. If the child has been used to spending holidays there, and he knows and is known by the staff, this crisis visit will not upset him as much as if he were going to strange people in a strange place. There is no greater tragedy than the totally protected child who is suddenly placed in an alien environment.

Clubs and Organisations

Most parents find that regular contact with other parents, especially parents with a handicapped child, gives them valuable support, and their child benefits from meeting other children. The local library will have details of any clubs for mothers and toddlers in the area, and also have the address of the nearest branch secretary of any organisation which has been formed particularly for those suffering from the same condition as their child. (National addresses of many organisations are given at the end of this book.) By taking part in such organisations, parents will not only derive great personal benefit but can help other parents in a similar situation in their turn.

Most children derive nothing but benefit from attending a good playgroup. They have the opportunity to experiment with many materials that are not easy to accommodate at home, and to use large equipment that the average family cannot afford such as a climbing frame or a Wendy House. They are offered a range of toys and they meet a large number of people and children. One of the values of a playgroup is that it gives mother and child an opportunity to begin the process of short separation which will continue when the child goes to school. It is especially important in helping him to learn to get on with adults other than his parents in unfamiliar surroundings. He will also have a gradual introduction to the school environment by being in a room much larger than those at home, and by being a member of a group rather than an individual. Because the playgroup can offer a high level of parental involvement, the child can come to terms with the new environment in his own time. The child who has never been exposed to similar surroundings or separated from his mother will be seriously upset on his first day at school. The health visitor may be able to advise on a good playgroup, and if parents have any doubts about their child's needs or his acceptance into such a group, the occupational therapist is the person to approach. She should be able to advise both the parents and the playgroup supervisor.

Playgroups are normally held on a part-time basis. Nurseries may be full time or part time and provide another stepping stone to full-time education. Schooling occupies a large portion of a child's life and much of his waking hours, and part of his success there will be due to adequate preparation. The gradual experiencing of separation is important, but a degree of personal independence is also desirable. His teachers should be fully informed of the child's condition, his needs, and his level of independence so that they will not expect too much — or too little — of him at first. It is a help for them to know what social skills he has and how they can be built on at school.

The possibility of their child's going to a special school is something that parents often feel very negative about. The most important point for them to consider is: will this school offer the best opportunities and provide the best care for my child? They should bear in mind that special schools employ teachers who have had additional training in meeting the needs of special children and that classes are far smaller than those found in ordinary schools. The needs of the child, viewed in the light of parental preference and local provision, are the deciding factor. The Education Act of 1981 requires that local authorities consult fully with parents over such decisions.

Looking Forward to the Future

However vulnerable a handicapped child may seem, there are excellent prospects for his future. They are founded on such factors as the rapid progress being made in medical knowledge and expertise, increasing technical ability in the design and manufacture of items such as artificial limbs and communication aids, and the great improvements made recently in public awareness and social acceptance. Advances in the ability to alleviate, if not eliminate, the problems which a handicapped child must face will come. It is up to us, the parents and those people who try to support them, to ensure that each child is able to benefit from such advances.

Useful Addresses

INVALID CHILDREN'S AID
ASSOCIATION
126 Buckingham Palace Road,
London, SW1W 9SB
Telephone: 01-730 9891

LADY HOARE TRUST FOR
PHYSICALLY DISABLED
CHILDREN
7 North Street
Midhurst
West Sussex GU29 9DJ
Telephone: 073-081 3696

NATIONAL ASSOCIATION FOR
THE WELFARE OF CHILDREN IN
HOSPITAL
7 Exton Street
London SE1
Telephone: 01-261 1738

VOLUNTARY COUNCIL FOR
HANDICAPPED CHILDREN
National Children's Bureau
8 Wakley Street
London EC1V 7QE
Telephone: 01-278 9441

NATIONAL SOCIETY FOR
AUTISTIC CHILDREN
1a Golders Green Road
London NW11 8EA
Telephone: 01-458 4375

CYSTIC FIBROSIS RESEARCH
TRUST
5 Blyth Road,
Bromley
Kent BR1 3RS
Telephone: 01-464 7211

NATIONAL DEAF CHILDREN'S
SOCIETY
31 Gloucester Place
London W1H 4EA
Telephone: 01-486 3251/2

DOWN'S CHILDREN'S
ASSOCIATION
Quinborne Community Centre
Ridgacre Road
Quinton
Birmingham B32 2TW
Telephone: 021-427 1374

MUSCULAR DYSTROPHY GROUP
OF GREAT BRITAIN
35 Macaulay Road,
London SW4 0QP
Telephone: 01-720 8055

ASSOCIATION FOR ALL SPEECH
IMPAIRED CHILDREN (AFASIC)
Room 14
Toynbee Hall
28 Commercial Street
London E1 6LS
Telephone: 01-247 1497

ASSOCIATION FOR SPINA BIFIDA
AND HYDROCEPHALUS (ASBAH)
Tavistock House North
Tavistock Square
London WC1H 9HJ
Telephone: 01-388 1382

TUBEROUS SCLEROSIS
ASSOCIATION OF GREAT
BRITAIN
c/o Church Farm House
Church Road, North Leigh
Oxfordshire OX8 6TX
Telephone: 0993-88 1238

ACTIVE
c/o Honorary Secretary
365 Burnt Oak Lane
Sidcup, Kent
(For play materials and communication
aids)

PRE-SCHOOL PLAYGROUPS
ASSOCIATION (PPA)
Alford House, Aveline Street
London SE11 5DH
Telephone: 01-582 8871 or
            01-582 8920

TOY LIBRARIES ASSOCIATION
Seabrook House
Wyllyots Manor
Darkes Lane, Potters Bar
Hertfordshire EN6 2HL
Telephone: 0707 44571

BREAK
20 Hooks Hill Road
Sheringham
Norfolk NR26 8NL
Telephone: 0263 823170 or
            0263 832025
(For holidays)

HANDICAPPED CHILDREN'S
PILGRIMAGE TRUST
95 Carshalton Road
Sutton
Surrey
Telephone: 01-643 4431

TRELOAR TRUST
Lord Mayor Treloar College
Froyle House
Froyle
near Alton
Hampshire GU34 4JX
Telephone: 04204 2199 and
            04204 2442
(Educates and trains physically
handicapped children between 9 and 19
years)

FAMILY FUND
PO Box 50
York YO3 6RB
Telephone: 0904 29241
(Helps families with severely
handicapped children to meet
essential needs not covered by other
services)

Recommended Reading

For Children

Title: *Rachel*
Author: Elizabeth Fanshawe
Publisher: Bodley Head

Title: *Miffy in Hospital*
Author: Dick Bruna
Publisher: Methuen Children's Books

Title: *Mark's Wheelchair Adventures*
Author: Camilla Jessel
Publisher: Methuen Children's Books

Title: *Paul in Hospital*
Author: Camilla Jessel
Publisher: Methuen Children's Books

Title: *Just Me*
Author: Jean Turnbull
Publisher: King Edward's Hospital Fund for London

Title: *Thomas Goes to the Doctor*
Author: Gunilla Wolde
Publisher: Hodder & Stoughton

Title: *Going into Hospital*
Author: Althea
Publisher: Dinosaur Publications Limited

Title: *Going to the Doctor*
Author: Althea
Publisher: Dinosaur Publications Limited

Title: *Visiting the Dentist*
Author: Althea
Publisher: Dinosaur Publications Limited

For Parents

Title: *Clothing for the Spina Bifida Child*
Author: Barbara Webster
Publisher: Association for Spina Bifida and Hydrocephalus

Title: *Clothing for the Handicapped Child*
Author: Gillian Forbes
Publisher: Disabled Living Foundation

Title: *Superwoman*
Author: Shirley Conran
Publisher: Penguin Books

Title: *Baby Shock*
Author: John Cobb
Publisher: Hutchinson

Title: *Toys and Play for the Handicapped Child*
Author: Barbara Riddick
Publisher: Croom Helm

Title: *Choosing Toys and Activities for Handicapped Children*
Author: Jill Norris
Publisher: Noah's ark publication

Title: *Help Your Child to Learn at Home*
Author: Victoria Shennan
Publisher: National Society for Mentally Handicapped Children

Title: *Equipment and Aids to Mobility*
Publisher: Association for Spina Bifida and Hydrocephalus

Title: *Living with Muscular Dystrophy*
Author: D. Collette Welch
Publisher: Muscular Dystrophy Group of Great Britain

Title: *Furniture for Children*
Author: Brian Brooks
Publisher: Evans Books

Title: *Bernard — Bringing Up our Mongol Son*
Author: John and Eileen Wilks
Publisher: Routledge & Kegan Paul

Title: *Let Me Play*
Author: Jeffree/McConkey/Hewson
Publisher: Souvenir Press

Title: *Reflection — A Book for Mums*
Author: Katherine Short
Publisher: Lion Publishing, Tring, Herts

Title: *How to Survive Children*
Author: Katherine Whitehorn
Publisher: Eyre Methuen

Title: *Easy to Make Aids for Your Handicapped Child*
Author: Don Caston
Publisher: Souvenir Press

Title: *Helping the Handicapped Child in the Family*
Author: Megan Jobling
Publisher: NFER/Nelson

Title: *Children about the House*
Author: Hilary Gelson
Publisher: Design Council

Title: *Clothing for the Handicapped Child*
Author: Gillian Forbes
Publisher: The Disabled Living Foundation

Title: *Toys and Playthings*
Author: John and Elizabeth Newson
Publisher: Penguin Books

Title: *The Pre-school Book*
Author: Brenda Thompson
Publisher: Sidgwick & Jackson

For Parents of Older Children

Title: *Growing up with Spina Bifida*
Author: Olwen Nettles
Publisher: Scottish Spina Bifida Association

Title: *What to Do When 'There's Nothing to Do'*
Author: Elizabeth M. Gregg
Publisher: Boston Children's Medical Centre. Arrow Books Limited

Title: *Gardening with Children*
Author: Alison Ross
Publisher: Faber & Faber

Title: *Learning to Cope*
Author: Edward Whelan/Barbara Speake
Publisher: Souvenir Press

For Professionals

Title: *Teaching the Handicapped Child*
Author: Jeffree/McConkey/Hewson
Publisher: Souvenir Press

Title: *Deprivation and Handicap*
Author: Wilson/Duncan/Mellor/ Sawbridge
Publisher: Institute of Mental Subnormality

Title: *Children's Developmental Progress*
Author: Mary D. Sheridan
Publisher: NFER/Nelson

Title: *The Handicapped Person In The Community*
Author: Boswell/Wingrove
Publisher: Tavistock Publications

Title: *Rehabilitation of Arm Amputees and Limb Deficient Children*
Author: Elizabeth Robertson
Publisher: Bailliere Tindall

Title: *Environmental Design for Handicapped Children*
Author: Sandhu/Hendriks-Jansen
Publisher: Saxon House

Title: *Some Mothers I Know*
Author: Tom Wakefield
Publisher: Routledge & Kegan Paul

Title: *Early Years*
Author: Morigue Cornwell
Publisher: Disabled Living Foundation

Title: *Physically Handicapped Children*
Author: Eugene E. Bleck and Donald A. Nagel
Publisher: Grune and Stratton

Title: *Equipment for the Disabled*
Publisher: 2 Foredown Drive, Portslade, Sussex BN4 2BB

Title: *The Dying Child*
Author: Jo-Eileen Gyulay
Publisher: McGraw-Hill Book Company

Title: *More Than Sympathy*
Author: Richard Lansdown
Publisher: Tavistock Publications Limited

Title: *Paediatric Assessment of Self-care Activities*
Author: Ida Lou Coley
Publisher: The C.V. Mosby Company, St Louis, USA

Title: *Mental Handicap Nursing and Care*
Author: Victoria Shannan
Publisher: Souvenir Press

Title: *Handicapped Children*
Author: John D. Kershaw
Publisher: William Heinemann Medical Books

Title: *Children with Spina Bifida at School*
Publisher: Association for Spina Bifida and Hydrocephalus

Title: *The Child*
Author: John Rendle-Short
Publisher: John Wright and Sons

Title: *Helping Your Handicapped Baby*
Author: Cliff Cunningham and Patricia Sloper
Publisher: Souvenir Press

Title: *Encouraging Language Development*
Author: Phyllis Hastings and Bessie Hayes
Publisher: Croom Helm

About the Author

Diana Millard is the District Occupational Therapist for the Peterborough Health Authority with responsibility for the management of the Occupational Therapy Service in the hospitals and units which form the Peterborough Health District. She is State registered and holds the Diploma of the College of Occupational Therapists. Trained at St Loye's, Exeter, she has had 14 years' clinical experience. Her career was temporarily set aside during her children's early years, but the insight gained at that time into the ramifications of child-rearing has proved invaluable in the development of her work with the families of handicapped children. She belongs to several organisations concerned with the welfare of children, and is a member of Soroptimist International.

Acknowledgements

I should like to thank Bill Gillham, the series editor, for inviting me to write this book; Sam Grainger, who took the photographs; Maria Majewska, the artist, who improved on my sketches; Marianne Thorpe and Diane Thurlow for assistance in typing the manuscript, and Muriel Deering, my mother, who helped me to check it; the Bedkowski, Forth, King, Millard and Walker families who were such willing and delightful models for the photographs; and above all my husband, Ian, and our daughters, Hazel and Heather, for their loving assistance.

D.M.

The author has been requested to state that the views expressed in this book are not necessarily those of the Peterborough Health Authority.

Index